Private Pilot

ORAL EXAM GUIDE

MICHAEL D. HAYES

ELEVENTH EDITION

THE COMPREHENSIVE GUIDE
TO PREPARE YOU FOR THE FAA
CHECKRIDE

Aviation Supplies & Academics, Inc.
Newcastle, Washington

Private Pilot Oral Exam Guide
Eleventh Edition
by Michael D. Hayes

Aviation Supplies & Academics, Inc.
7005 132nd Place SE
Newcastle, Washington 98059-3153

Visit ASA's website often (**www.asa2fly.com**) to find updates posted there due to FAA regulation revisions that may affect this book. See also **www.asa2fly.com/reader/oegp** for the "Reader Resources" page with additional information and updates.

Printed in the United States of America

2020   2019   2018   9 8 7 6 5 4 3

ASA-OEG-P11
ISBN   978-1-61954-459-8

Library of Congress Cataloging-in-Publication Data:

Hayes, Michael D.
   Private pilot oral exam guide: the comprehensive guide to prepare
you for the FAA checkride / by Michael D. Hayes.
         p.   cm.
   "ASA-OEG-P"—Cover.
   1. Aeronautics—Examinations, questions, etc. 2. Private
flying—Examinations, questions, etc. 3. United States. Federal
Aviation Administration—Examinations—Study guides.
4. Oral examinations. I. Aviation Supplies & Academics, Inc.
II. Title.
TL546.5.H33   1993   93-12050
   629.132'5217'076—dc20   CIP

03

This guide is dedicated to the many talented students, pilots and flight instructors I have had the opportunity to work with over the years. Also, special thanks to Mark Hayes and many others who supplied the patience, encouragement, and understanding necessary to complete the project.

—M.D.H.

Contents

Introduction

The *Private Oral Exam Guide* is a comprehensive guide designed
for student pilots who are involved in training for the Private Pilot
Certificate. This guide was originally designed for use in a 14 CFR
Part 141 flight school but has quickly become popular with those
training under Part 61 and are not affiliated with an FAA-approved
school. The guide will also prove beneficial to private pilots who wish
to refresh their knowledge or who are preparing for a flight review.

The Private Pilot Airplane Airman Certification Standards
(FAA-S-ACS-6) specifies the areas in which knowledge must be
demonstrated by the applicant before a pilot certificate or rating can be
issued. The *Private Oral Exam Guide* has been designed to evaluate
a pilot's knowledge of those areas. This guide contains questions
and answers organized into eight main divisions which represent
those areas of knowledge required for the practical test. Check the
ASA website (**www.asa2fly.com** and dedicated Reader Resource
page for this book **www.asa2fly.com/reader/oegp**) periodically for
downloadable Updates, which are created whenever changes occur in
FAA regulations and procedures affecting this book; future Updates
may also contain additional study material and new FAA information
regarding the Private Pilot checkride.

At any time during the practical test, an FAA examiner may ask
questions pertaining to any of the subject areas within these divisions.
In addition, Chapter 9 provides scenario-based questions which often
test multiple subjects or areas. Through very intensive post-private
pilot checkride debriefings, we have provided you with the most
consistent questions asked along with the information necessary for a
knowledgeable response. The guide may be supplemented with other
comprehensive study materials as noted in parentheses after each
question. For example: (FAA-H-8083-3). The abbreviations for these
materials and their titles are listed below. Be sure to use the latest
revision of these references when reviewing for the test.

AC 120-27	*Aircraft Weight and Balance Control*
FAA-H-8083-1	*Aircraft Weight & Balance Handbook*
FAA-H-8083-2	*Risk Management Handbook*
FAA-H-8083-3	*Airplane Flying Handbook*
FAA-H-8083-6	*Advanced Avionics Handbook*
FAA-H-8083-9	*Aviation Instructor's Handbook*
FAA-H-8083-15	*Instrument Flying Handbook*
FAA-H-8083-16	*Instrument Procedures Handbook*
FAA-H-8083-19	*Plane Sense: General Aviation Information*
FAA-H-8083-25	*Pilot's Handbook of Aeronautical Knowledge*
FAA-H-8083-30	*Aviation Maintenance Technician Handbook— General*
FAA-P-8740-2	*Density Altitude*
FAA-P-8740-35	*All About Fuel*
FAA-P-8740-36	*Proficiency and the Private Pilot*
FAA-P-8740-41	*Medical Facts for Pilots*
FAA-P-8740-69	*Aeronautical Decision Making*
FAA-S-ACS-6	*Private Pilot Airplane Airman Certification Standards*
AFM	*FAA-Approved Airplane Flight Manual*
AIM	*Aeronautical Information Manual*
AWC	*Aviation Weather Center (internet)*
CSUS	*Chart Supplement U.S.*
FAA Safety	*"General Aviation Pilot's Guide to Preflight Weather Planning, Weather Self-Briefings, and Weather Decision Making"*
FAA Safety ALC-25	*Flight Reveiw Prep Guide*
FSSAT	*Flight School Security Awareness Training*
Order 8900.1	*Flight Standards Information Management System*
POH	*Pilot Operating Handbook*
SAIB CE-11-17	*Instruments (Maneuvering Speed)*
SAFO	*FAA Safety Alert for Operators*
SAFO 11004	*Runway Incursion Prevention Actions*
TSA	*Transportation Security Admninistration*
USRGD	*FAA Aeronautical Chart User's Guide*

These documents are available from **www.faa.gov**. Additionally, many of the publications are reprinted by ASA and are available from aviation retailers nationwide.

A review of the information presented within this guide should provide the necessary preparation for the FAA Private Pilot Certification Practical test.

Pilot
Qualifications

1

A. Privileges and Limitations

1. What are the eligibility requirements for a private pilot (airplane) certificate? (14 CFR 61.103)

a. Be at least 17 years of age.

b. Be able to read, speak, write, and understand the English language.

c. Hold at least a current Third Class medical certificate.

d. Received the required ground and flight training endorsements.

e. Meet the applicable aeronautical experience requirements.

f. Passed the required knowledge and practical tests.

Exam Tip: The evaluator may ask you to demonstrate that you're current and eligible to take the practical test. When preparing for your practical test, verify that you have the required hours, that you're current, and don't forget to double-check all of your endorsements (especially the 90-day solo flight endorsement). Make sure you have totaled all of the logbook columns and that the entries make sense.

2. What privileges and limitations apply to a private pilot? (14 CFR 61.113)

No person who holds a private pilot certificate may act as pilot in command of an aircraft that is carrying passengers or property for compensation or hire; nor may that person, for compensation or hire, act as pilot in command of an aircraft. A private pilot—

a. May act as PIC of an aircraft in connection with any business or employment if it is only incidental to that business or employment and does not carry passengers or property for compensation or hire.

b. May not pay less than the pro rata share of the operating expenses of a flight with passengers, provided the expenses involve only fuel, oil, airport expenditures, or rental fees.

c. May act as PIC of a charitable, nonprofit, or community event flight described in 14 CFR §91.146, if the sponsor and pilot comply with the requirements of that regulation.

Continued

    d. May be reimbursed for aircraft operating expenses that are directly related to search and location operations, provided the expenses involve only fuel, oil, airport expenditures, or rental fees, and the operation is sanctioned and under the direction and control of local, state, or Federal agencies or organizations that conduct search and location operations.

    e. May demonstrate an aircraft in flight to a prospective buyer if the private pilot is an aircraft salesman and has at least 200 hours of logged flight time.

    f. May act as PIC of an aircraft towing a glider or unpowered ultralight vehicle, provided they meet the requirements of 14 CFR §61.69.

    g. May act as PIC for the purpose of conducting a production flight test in a light-sport aircraft intended for certification in the light-sport category, provided they meet the requirements of 14 CFR §21.190.

3. Explain the statement "may not pay less than pro-rata share of the operating expenses of a flight."
(14 CFR 61.113)

Pro-rata means "proportional." The pilot may not pay less than his or her proportional share of the flight's operating expenses with the passengers, provided the expenses involve only fuel, oil, airport expenditures or rental fees.

4. The annual inspection for your aircraft is now due and you ask several friends that fly with you regularly to contribute money to help you pay for the inspection. Do the regulations allow for these contributions?
(14 CFR 61.113)

No. A private pilot may not pay less than the pro rata (proportional) share of the operating expenses of a flight with passengers, provided the expenses involve only fuel, oil, airport expenditures or rental fees.

Note: The regulation applies to "the operating expenses of a flight," and does not allow for the sharing of fixed or long term operating costs of the airplane with passengers.

5. **To act as a required pilot flight crewmember of a civil aircraft, what must a pilot have in his/her physical possession or readily accessible in the aircraft?** (14 CFR 61.3)

   a. A pilot certificate (or special purpose pilot authorization)

   b. A photo identification

   c. A medical certificate (with certain exceptions as provided in 14 CFR §61.3)

6. **While you are performing a preflight inspection on your aircraft, an inspector from the FAA introduces herself and says she wants to conduct a ramp inspection. What documents are you required to show the inspector?** (14 CFR 61.3)

   Each person who holds an airman certificate, medical certificate, authorization, or license required by 14 CFR part 61 must present it and their photo identification for inspection upon a request from the administrator, an authorized NTSB representative, any federal, state, or local law enforcement officer, or an authorized representative of the TSA.

7. **What is the definition of a high-performance airplane, and what must you do to act as pilot-in-command of such an airplane?** (14 CFR 61.31)

   A high-performance is an airplane with an engine of more than 200 horsepower. To act as PIC of a high-performance you must have:

   a. Received and logged ground and flight training from an authorized instructor in a high-performance airplane, or in a flight simulator or flight training device that is representative of a high-performance airplane, and have been found proficient in the operation and systems of that airplane.

   b. Received and logged a one-time endorsement in your logbook from an authorized instructor who certifies you are proficient to operate a high-performance airplane.

   Note: The training and endorsement required by this regulation is not required if the person has logged flight time as PIC of a high-performance airplane, or in a flight simulator or flight training device that is representative of a high-performance airplane prior to August 4, 1997.

8. Other than high-performance and complex aircraft, what other types of aircraft (ASEL) require specific training and logbook endorsements from an appropriately rated flight instructor? (14 CFR 61.31)

High-Altitude Airplane—No person may act as pilot-in-command of a pressurized airplane that has a service ceiling or maximum operating altitude (whichever is lower), above 25,000 feet MSL unless that person has completed the ground and flight training specified and has received a logbook or training record endorsement from an authorized instructor certifying satisfactory completion of the training.

Tailwheel Airplane—No person may act as pilot-in-command of a tailwheel airplane unless that person has received and logged flight training from an authorized instructor in a tailwheel airplane and received an endorsement in the person's logbook from an authorized instructor who found the person proficient in the operation of a tailwheel airplane. The training and endorsement is not required if the person logged pilot-in-command time in a tailwheel airplane before April 15, 1991.

9. What is the definition of a complex airplane, and what must you do to act as pilot-of-command of such an airplane? (14 CFR 61.1, 14 CFR 61.31)

A "complex airplane" is defined as an airplane that has a retractable landing gear, flaps, and a controllable pitch propeller; including airplanes equipped with a full-authority digital engine control (FADEC). To act as pilot-in-command of such an airplane, you must have:

a. Received and logged ground and flight training from an authorized instructor in a complex airplane, or in a flight simulator or flight training device that is representative of a complex airplane and have been found proficient in the operation and systems of the airplane.

b. Received a one-time endorsement in your logbook from an authorized instructor who certifies you are proficient to operate a complex airplane.

Note: The training and endorsement required by this regulation is not required if the person has logged flight time as PIC of a complex airplane, or in a flight simulator or flight training device that is representative of a complex airplane prior to August 4, 1997.

10. With respect to certification, privileges, and limitations of airmen, define the terms: "Category," "Class," and "Type." (14 CFR Part 1)

Category—a broad classification of aircraft; i.e., airplane, rotorcraft, glider, etc.

Class—a classification of aircraft within a category having similar operating characteristics; i.e., single-engine land, multi-engine land; etc.

Type—a specific make and basic model of aircraft including modifications that do not change its handling or flight characteristics; i.e., DC-9, B-737, C-150, etc.

B. Currency Requirements

1. What are the requirements to remain current as a private pilot? (14 CFR 61.56, 61.57)

a. Within the preceding 24 months, accomplished a flight review given in an aircraft for which that pilot is rated by an authorized instructor and received a logbook endorsement certifying that the person has satisfactorily completed the review.

b. To carry passengers, a pilot must have made, within the preceding 90 days –

- three takeoffs and landings as the sole manipulator of flight controls of an aircraft of the same category and class and, if a type rating is required, of the same type.
- if the aircraft is a tailwheel airplane, the landings must have been made to a full stop in an airplane with a tailwheel.
- if operations are to be conducted during the period beginning 1 hour after sunset and 1 hour before sunrise, with passengers on board, the PIC must have, within the preceding 90 days, made at least three takeoffs and three landings to a full stop during that period in an aircraft of the same category, class, and type (if a type is required), of aircraft to be used.

Note: Takeoffs and landings required by this regulation may be accomplished in a flight simulator or flight training device that is approved by the Administrator and used in accordance with an approved course conducted by a certificated training center.

2. **You have not kept up with logging each of your recent flights. Are you in violation of any regulation?** (14 CFR 61.51)

No. You're only required to document and record the training and aeronautical experience used to meet the requirements for a certificate, rating, or flight review, and the aeronautical experience required for meeting the recent flight experience requirements.

3. **You're flying in a single-engine, high performance, complex airplane. You hold a Private Pilot certificate with an airplane single-engine land rating, but don't have a high-performance or complex airplane endorsement. Your friend, who has those endorsements, is acting as PIC for the flight. Can you log PIC time for the time you act as sole manipulator of the controls? Explain.** (14 CFR 61.31, 61.51)

Yes, 14 CFR 61.51 governs the logging of pilot-in-command (PIC) time and states that a sport, recreational, private, commercial, or airline transport pilot may log PIC time for the time during which that pilot is "sole manipulator of the controls of an aircraft for which the pilot is rated or has privileges."

Note: This means you can log PIC time, but you cannot act as PIC. For a pilot to act as PIC, he or she must be properly rated in the aircraft and authorized to conduct the flight which would include having the required endorsements for complex and high performance airplanes as required by 14 CFR 61.31.

4. **Explain the difference between being "current" and being "proficient."** (FAA-H-8083-2, FAA-P-8740-36)

Being "current" means that a pilot has accomplished the minimum FAA regulatory requirements within a specific time period so he or she can exercise the privileges of their certificate. It means that you're "legal" to make a flight, but does not necessarily mean that you're proficient or competent to make that flight.

Being "proficient" means that a pilot is capable of conducting a flight with a high degree of competence; it requires that the pilot must have a wide range of knowledge and skills. Being proficient is not about just being "legal" in terms of the regulations, but is about being "smart" and "safe" in terms of pilot experience and proficiency.

5. How will establishing a personal minimums checklist reduce risk? (FAA-H-8083-25)

Professional pilots live by the numbers, and so should you. Pre-established numbers can make it a lot easier to come to a smart go/no-go or diversion decision, than would the vague sense that you can "probably" deal with the conditions you face at any given time. A written set of personal minimums also make it easier to explain tough cancelation or diversion decisions to passengers who are, after all, trusting their lives to your aeronautical skill and judgment.

6. The airplane you normally rent has been grounded due to an intermittent electrical problem. You ask to be scheduled in another airplane. During preflight of the new airplane, you discover that it has avionics you're unfamiliar with. Should you go ahead and depart on your VFR flight? (FAA-H-8083-2)

Pilot familiarity with all equipment is critical in optimizing both safety and efficiency. If a pilot is unfamiliar with any aircraft system, this will add to workload and can contribute to a loss of situational awareness. This level of proficiency is critical and should be looked upon as a requirement, not unlike carrying an adequate supply of fuel. As a result, pilots should not look upon unfamiliarity with the aircraft and its systems as a risk control measure, but instead as a hazard with high risk potential. Discipline is the key to success.

7. If a pilot changes his/her permanent mailing address and fails to notify the FAA Airmen Certification branch of the new address, how long may the pilot continue to exercise the privileges of his/her pilot certificate? (14 CFR 61.60)

30 days after the date of the move.

8. What flight time can a pilot log as second-in-command time? (14 CFR 61.51)

A person may log second-in-command (SIC) time only for that flight time during which that person:

a. Is qualified in accordance with the SIC requirements of 14 CFR §61.55, and occupies a crewmember station in an aircraft that requires more than one pilot by the aircraft's type certificate; or

b. Holds the appropriate category, class, and instrument rating (if an instrument rating is required for the flight) for the aircraft being flown, and more than one pilot is required under the type certification of the aircraft or the regulations under which the flight is being conducted.

C. Medical Certificates

1. To exercise the privileges of a private pilot certificate, what medical certificate is required, and how long is it valid? (14 CFR 61.23, 14 CFR Part 68)

You must hold at least a third-class medical certificate. The medical certificate expires at the end of the last day of:

a. The 60th month after the month of the date of examination shown on the certificate, if on the date of your most recent medical examination you were under the age of 40.

b. The 24th month after the month of the date of examination shown on the certificate, if on the date of your most recent medical examination you were over the age of 40.

Note: Third class medical reform went into effect in 2017, eliminating the need for a third class medical certificate for many. Visit www.faa.gov for updates on this Part 68 "BasicMed."

2. **Spring has finally arrived and the weather looks great so you decide to rent an airplane and go fly. The problem is, your allergies are giving you a problem and you have just taken your medication. Can you still go fly? Explain.** (14 CFR 61.53, 91.17, FAA-H-8083-25)

The safest rule is not to fly while taking any medication, unless approved to do so by the FAA. Some of the most commonly used over-the-counter (OTC) drugs, antihistamines and decongestants, have the potential to cause noticeable adverse side effects, including drowsiness and cognitive deficits. 14 CFR prohibits pilots from performing crewmember duties while using any medication that affects the body in any way contrary to safety. If there is any doubt regarding the effects of any medication, consult an Aviation Medical Examiner (AME) before flying.

3. **Where can you find a list of the medical conditions that may disqualify you from obtaining a medical certificate?** (14 CFR Part 67, FAA-H-8083-25)

The standards for medical certification are contained in 14 CFR Part 67 and the requirements for obtaining medical certificates can be found in 14 CFR Part 61.

Additional Study Questions

1. One way a pilot can limit exposure to risks is to set personal minimums for items in each risk category (PAVE). Describe the individual minimums you will establish for yourself. (FAA-H-8083-2)

2. As a newly certificated private pilot, you are ready to utilize your certificate. I'm a friend and need you to fly a package to a distant destination. I will pay for the airplane if you accept. Do the regulations allow you to accept the offer? (14 CFR 61.113)

3. For a person under the age of 40, when will a third class medical certificate issued on March 15, 2016 expire? (14 CFR 61.60)

4. What are some examples of general medical conditions that are temporarily disqualifying? (AIM 8-1-1, 14 CFR 61.53)

5. If your driver's license was recently suspended for driving under the influence of alcohol (DUI), but you have not been actually convicted of the crime, must you report this to the FAA? (14 CFR 61.15)

6. You have allowed over 24 months to lapse since your last flight review. Is your Private Pilot Certificate now invalid? What do you have to do to be legal to fly again? (14 CFR 61.19, 14 CFR 61.56)

7. Are there any other activities a pilot can accomplish that can be substituted for a flight review? (14 CFR 61.56)

8. What regulatory requirements must be met prior to a pilot acting as PIC of an aircraft towing a glider? (14 CFR 61.69)

Airworthiness
Requirements

2

A. Aircraft Certificates and Documents

1. What documents are required on board an aircraft prior to flight? (14 CFR 91.203, 91.9)

A irworthiness Certificate (14 CFR 91.203)

R egistration Certificate (14 CFR 91.203)

R adio Station License (if operating outside of U.S.; an FCC regulation)

O perating Limitations—AFM/POH and supplements, placards, markings (14 CFR 91.9)

W eight and balance data (current)

Compass Deviation Card (14 CFR 23.1547)

External Data Plate/Serial Number (14 CFR 45.11)

Exam Tip: During the practical test your evaluator may wish to examine the various required aircraft documents (ARROW) during the preflight inspection, as well as the currency of any aeronautical charts, EFB data, etc. on board the aircraft. Prior to the test, verify that all of the necessary aircraft documentation, on-board databases and charts are current and available.

2. What is an airworthiness certificate? (FAA-H-8083-25)

An airworthiness certificate is issued by the FAA to an aircraft that has been proven to meet the minimum design and manufacturing requirements and is condition for safe operation. Under any circumstances, the aircraft must meet the requirements of the original type certificate or it is no longer airworthy. These certificates come in two different classifications: standard airworthiness and special airworthiness.

3. What is the difference between standard and special airworthiness certificates? (FAA-H-8083-25)

Standard airworthiness certificates (white paper) are issued for normal, utility, acrobatic, commuter, or transport category aircraft. Special airworthiness certificates (pink paper) are issued for primary, restricted, or limited category aircraft, and light sport aircraft.

4. What is an experimental airworthiness certificate? (FAA-H-8083-25)

A special airworthiness certificate in the experimental category is issued to operate an aircraft that does not have a type certificate or does not conform to its type certificate yet is in a condition for safe operation. Additionally, this certificate is issued to operate a primary category kit-built aircraft that was assembled without the supervision and quality control of the production certificate holder.

5. Does an airworthiness certificate have an expiration date? (FAA-H-8083-25)

No. A standard airworthiness certificate remains valid for as long as the aircraft meets its approved type design, is in a condition for safe operation, and the maintenance, preventative maintenance, and alterations are performed in accordance with 14 CFR Parts 21, 43, and 91.

6. Where must the airworthiness certificate be located? (14 CFR 91.203, FAA-H-8083-19)

The certificate must be displayed at the cabin or cockpit entrance so that it is legible to passengers or crew.

7. For an aircraft to be considered airworthy, what two conditions must be met? (FAA-H-8083-19)

a. The aircraft must conform to its type design (type certificate). This is attained when the required and proper components are installed consistent with the drawings, specifications, and other data that are part of the type certificate. Conformity includes applicable supplemental type certificate(s) (STC) and field-approval alterations.

b. The aircraft must be in a condition for safe operation, referring to the condition of the aircraft in relation to wear and deterioration.

8. **Explain how a pilot determines if an aircraft conforms to its approved type design and is in a condition for safe operation.** (14 CFR Part 21)

   a. For type design, a pilot must determine that the maintenance, preventive maintenance, and alterations have been performed in accordance 14 CFR Parts 21, 43, and 91 and that the aircraft is registered in the U.S. The pilot does this by ensuring that all required inspections, maintenance, preventive maintenance, repairs and alterations have been appropriately documented in the aircraft's maintenance records.

   b. For safe operation, the pilot conducts a thorough preflight inspection of the aircraft for wear and deterioration, structural damage, fluid leaks, tire wear, inoperative instruments and equipment, etc. If an unsafe condition exists or inoperative instruments or equipment are found, the pilot uses the guidance in 14 CFR 91.213 for handling the inoperative equipment.

9. **What records or documents should be checked to determine that the owner or operator of an aircraft has complied with all required inspections and airworthiness directives?** (14 CFR 91.405)

   The maintenance records (aircraft and engine logbooks). Each owner or operator of an aircraft shall ensure that maintenance personnel make appropriate entries in the aircraft maintenance records indicating the aircraft has been approved for return to service.

10. **Who is responsible for ensuring that an aircraft is maintained in an airworthy condition?** (14 CFR 91.403)

    The owner or operator of an aircraft is primarily responsible for maintaining an aircraft in an airworthy condition.

11. **Describe some of the responsibilities an aircraft owner has pertaining to aircraft documents, maintenance, and inspections of their aircraft?** (FAA-H-8083-25)

    Aircraft owners must:

    a. Have a current airworthiness certificate and aircraft registration in the aircraft.

Continued

b. Maintain the aircraft in an airworthy condition including compliance with all applicable Airworthiness Directives.

c. Ensure maintenance is properly recorded.

d. Keep abreast of current regulations concerning the operation of that aircraft.

e. Notify the FAA Civil Aviation Registry immediately of any change of permanent mailing address, or of the sale or export of the aircraft, or of the loss of citizenship.

f. Have a current FCC radio station license if equipped with radios, including emergency locator transmitter (ELT), if operated outside of the United States.

12. What are "airworthiness directives"? (FAA-H-8083-25)

An airworthiness directive (AD) is the medium by which the FAA notifies aircraft owners and other potentially interested persons of unsafe conditions that may exist because of design defects, maintenance, or other causes, and specifies the conditions under which the product may continue to be operated. ADs are regulatory in nature, and compliance is mandatory. It is the aircraft owner's or operator's responsibility to ensure compliance with all pertinent ADs.

13. What are the two types of ADs? (FAA-H-8083-19)

ADs are divided into two categories: Those of an emergency nature requiring immediate compliance prior to further flight, and those of a less urgent nature requiring compliance within a specified period of time.

14. When are emergency ADs issued? (FAA-H-8083-19)

An emergency AD is issued when an unsafe condition exists that requires immediate action by an owner/operator. The intent of an emergency AD is to rapidly correct an urgent safety-of-flight situation. All known owners and operators of affected U.S.-registered aircraft or those aircraft that have an affected product installed will be sent a copy of an emergency AD.

Exam Tip: ADs and recurring ADs—Be capable of finding and explaining the status of all ADs and recurring ADs that exist for your aircraft. Locate and tab prior to the practical test.

15. What is a type certificate data sheet? (FAA-H-8083-30)

The FAA issues a type certificate when a new aircraft, engine, propeller, etc., is found to meet safety standards set forth by the FAA. The type certificate data sheet (TCDS) lists the specifications, conditions and limitations under which airworthiness requirements were met for the specified product, such as engine make and model, fuel type, engine limits, airspeed limits, maximum weight, minimum crew, etc.

16. What is a supplemental type certificate? (FAA-H-8083-3, FAA-H-8083-30, AC 21-40)

A supplemental type certificate (STC) is the FAA's approval of a major change in the type design of a previously approved type certificated product. The certificate authorizes an alteration to an airframe, engine, or component that has been granted an approved type certificate. Sometimes alterations are made that are not specified or authorized in the TCDS. When that condition exists, an STC will be issued. STCs are considered a part of the permanent records of an aircraft, and should be maintained as part of that aircraft's logs.

17. What is an aircraft registration certificate? (FAA-H-8083-25)

Before an aircraft can be flown legally, it must be registered with the FAA Aircraft Registry. The Certificate of Aircraft Registration, which is issued to the owner as evidence of the registration, must be carried in the aircraft at all times.

18. Does an aircraft's registration certificate have an expiration date? (14 CFR 47.31, 47.40)

Yes. A Certificate of Aircraft Registration issued in accordance with 14 CFR §47.31 expires three years after the last day of the month in which it was issued. A temporary certification of registration is valid for no more than 90 days after the date the applicant signs the application.

19. Where can you find information on the placards and marking information required to be in the airplane? (FAA-H-8083-25, AC 60-6, 14 CFR 91.9, 14 CFR 23.1541)

The principle source of information for identifying the required Airplane Flight Manuals, approved manual materials, markings, and placards is the FAA type certificate data sheet or aircraft specification issued for each airplane eligible for an airworthiness certificate. The required placards are also reproduced in the "Limitations" section of the AFM or as directed by an AD.

20. What are several examples of placards and markings required in the airplane? (14 CFR 23.1545 through 23.1567)

Placards—Day-Night-VFR-IFR placard, "Flight Maneuvers Permitted" placard, "Caution Control Lock Remove before Starting," "Maneuvering Speed," "Compass Calibration Card," etc.

Markings—Airspeed indicator markings, cockpit control markings, fuel, oil, and coolant filler openings, etc.

B. Aircraft Maintenance Requirements

1. What are the required tests and inspections to be performed on an aircraft? Include inspections for IFR. (14 CFR 91.409, 91.171, 91.411, 91.413, 91.207)

A	Annual inspection within the preceding 12 calendar months (14 CFR 91.409)
A	Airworthiness directives and life-limited parts complied with, as required (14 CFR 91.403, 91.417)
V	VOR equipment check every 30 days (for IFR ops) (14 CFR 91.171)
1	100-hour inspection, if used for hire or flight instruction in aircraft CFI provides (14 CFR 91.409)
A	Altimeter, altitude reporting equipment, and static pressure systems tested and inspected (for IFR ops) every 24 calendar months (14 CFR 91.411)
T	Transponder tests and inspections, every 24 calendar months (14 CFR 91.413)
E	Emergency locator transmitter, operation and battery condition inspected every 12 calendar months (14 CFR 91.207)

Exam Tip: Be prepared to locate all of the required inspections, ADs, life-limited parts, etc. in the aircraft and engine logbooks and be able to determine when the next inspections are due. Create an aircraft status sheet that indicates the status of all required inspections, ADs, life limited, parts, etc. and/or use post-it notes to tab the specific pages in the aircraft and engine logbooks. Write the due date of the next inspection on the post-it note.

2. What is an "annual" inspection and which aircraft are required to have annual inspections? (FAA-H-8083-25)

An annual inspection is a complete inspection of an aircraft and engine, required by the regulations and is required to be accomplished every 12 calendar months on all certificated aircraft. Only an A&P technician holding an Inspection Authorization can conduct an annual inspection.

3. What aircraft are required to have 100-hour inspections? (FAA-H-8083-25, 14 CFR 91.409)

a. All aircraft under 12,500 pounds (except turbojet/ turbopropeller-powered multi-engine airplanes and turbine powered rotorcraft), used to carry passengers for hire.

b. Aircraft used for flight instruction for hire, when provided by the person giving the flight instruction.

4. If an aircraft is operated for hire, is it required to have a 100-hour inspection as well as an annual inspection? (14 CFR 91.409)

Yes, if an aircraft is operated for hire it must have a 100-hour inspection as well as an annual inspection when due. If not operated for hire, only an annual inspection is required.

5. What is the difference between an annual inspection and a 100-hour inspection? (14 CFR Part 43)

The main difference is who is allowed to perform these inspections. Only an A&P mechanic with an Inspection Authorization can perform an annual inspection. 100-hour inspections may be performed by any A&P mechanic (no IA required). 14 CFR Part 43, Appendix D ("Scope and Detail of Items to be Included in Annual and 100-Hour Inspections") contains a list of items to be checked during inspections.

6. **If an aircraft has been on a schedule of inspection every 100 hours, under what condition may it continue to operate beyond the 100 hours without a new inspection?** (14 CFR 91.409)

The 100-hour limitation may be exceeded by not more than 10 hours while en route to a place where the inspection can be done. The excess time used to reach a place where the inspection can be done must be included in computing the next 100 hours of time in service.

7. **If the annual inspection date has passed, can an aircraft be operated to a location where the inspection can be performed?** (FAA-H-8083-25)

An aircraft overdue for an annual inspection may be operated under a Special Flight Permit issued by the FAA for the purpose of flying the aircraft to a location where the annual inspection can be performed. However, all applicable ADs that are due must be complied with before the flight.

8. **What are "Special Flight Permits," and when are they necessary?** (14 CFR 91.213, 14 CFR 21.197)

A Special Flight Permit may be issued for an aircraft that may not currently meet applicable airworthiness requirements but is capable of safe flight. These permits are typically issued for the following purposes:

a. Flying an aircraft to a base where repairs, alterations or maintenance are to be performed, or to a point of storage.

b. Delivering or exporting an aircraft.

c. Production flight testing new-production aircraft.

d. Evacuating aircraft from areas of impending danger.

e. Conducting customer demonstration flights in new-production aircraft that have satisfactorily completed production flight tests.

9. How are "Special Flight Permits" obtained?
(FAA-H-8083-25)

If a special flight permit is needed, assistance and the necessary forms may be obtained from the local FSDO or Designated Airworthiness Representative (DAR).

10. After aircraft inspections have been made and defects have been repaired, who is responsible for determining that the aircraft is in an airworthy condition?
(14 CFR 91.7)

The pilot-in-command of a civil aircraft is responsible for determining whether that aircraft is in a condition for safe flight. The pilot-in-command shall discontinue the flight when un-airworthy, mechanical, electrical, or structural conditions occur.

11. What regulations apply concerning the operation of an aircraft that has had alterations or repairs which may have substantially affected its operation in flight? (14 CFR 91.407)

No person may operate or carry passengers in any aircraft that has undergone maintenance, preventative maintenance, rebuilding, or alteration that may have appreciably changed its flight characteristics or substantially affected its operation in flight until an appropriately-rated pilot with at least a private pilot certificate

a. Flies the aircraft;

b. Makes an operational check of the maintenance performed or alteration made; and

c. Logs the flight in the aircraft records.

12. Can a pilot legally conduct flight operations with known inoperative equipment onboard? (14 CFR 91.213, AC 91-67)

Yes, under specific conditions. 14 CFR Part 91 describes acceptable methods for the operation of an aircraft with certain inoperative instruments and equipment that are not essential for safe flight—they are:

Continued

a. Operation of an aircraft with a Minimum Equipment List (MEL), as authorized by 14 CFR 91.213(a) or -

b. Operation of an aircraft without a MEL under 14 CFR 91.213(d)

Exam Tip: Know this regulation well—unfamiliarity with 14 CFR 91.213 is a common weakness of applicants at all levels. You must demonstrate that you know this regulation and how to apply it.

13. What limitations apply to aircraft operations conducted using the deferral provision of 14 CFR 91.213(d)? (FAA-H-8083-25)

When inoperative equipment is found during preflight or prior to departure, the decision should be to cancel the flight, obtain maintenance prior to flight, or to defer the item or equipment. Maintenance deferrals are not used for inflight discrepancies. The manufacturer's AFM/POH procedures are to be used in those situations.

14. During the preflight inspection in an aircraft that doesn't have a MEL, you notice that an instrument or equipment item is inoperative. Describe how you will determine if the aircraft is still airworthy for flight. (14 CFR 91.213(d), AC 91-67, FAA-H-8083-25)

I will ask myself the following questions to determine if I can legally fly the airplane with the inoperative equipment item:

a. Are the inoperative instruments or equipment part of the VFR-day type certification?

b. Are the inoperative instruments or equipment listed as "Required" on the aircraft's equipment list or "Kinds of Operations Equipment List (KOEL)" for the type of flight operation being conducted?

c. Are the inoperative instruments or equipment required by 14 CFR §91.205, §91.207 or any other rule of 14 CFR Part 91 for the specific kind of flight operation being conducted? (For example, VFR, IFR, day, night.)

d. Are the inoperative instruments or equipment required to be operational by an AD?

If the answer is "Yes" to any of these questions, the aircraft is not airworthy and maintenance is required before I can fly. If the answer is "No" to any of these questions, then the inoperative instruments or equipment must be removed (by an A&P) from the aircraft, or deactivated and placarded "Inoperative."

Note: See Appendix 3 for further explanation of this regulation.

Exam Tip: If an instrument or equipment item is inoperative in your aircraft, be able to explain how you will determine if the aircraft is airworthy and legal for flight.

15. What are Minimum Equipment Lists? (AC 91-67)

The Minimum Equipment List (MEL) is a precise listing of instruments, equipment and procedures that allows an aircraft to be operated under specific conditions with inoperative equipment. The MEL is the specific inoperative equipment document for a particular make and model aircraft by serial and registration numbers; e.g., BE-200, N12345. The FAA-approved MEL includes only those items of equipment that the FAA deems may be inoperative and still maintain an acceptable level of safety with appropriate conditions and limitations.

Note: Do not confuse an MEL with the aircraft's equipment list. They are not the same.

16. For an aircraft with an approved MEL, explain the decision sequence a pilot would use after discovering the position lights are inoperative. (FAA-H-8083-25)

With an approved MEL, if the position lights were discovered inoperative prior to a daytime flight, the pilot would make an entry in the maintenance record or discrepancy record provided for that purpose. The item is then either repaired or deferred in accordance with the MEL. Upon confirming that daytime flight with inoperative position lights is acceptable in accordance with the provisions of the MEL, the pilot would leave the position lights switch OFF, open the circuit breaker (or whatever action is called for in the procedures document), and placard the position light switch as INOPERATIVE.

17. Explain the limitations that apply to aircraft operations being conducted using an MEL. (FAA-H-8083-25)

The use of an MEL for a small, non-turbine-powered airplane operated under Part 91 allows for the deferral of inoperative items or equipment. The FAA considers an approved MEL to be a supplemental type certificate (STC) issued to an aircraft by serial number and registration number. Once an operator requests an MEL, and a Letter of Authorization (LOA) is issued by the FAA, then the MEL becomes mandatory for that aircraft. All maintenance deferrals must be done in accordance with the terms and conditions of the MEL and the operator-generated procedures document.

18. What instruments and equipment are required for VFR day flight? (14 CFR 91.205)

For VFR flight during the day, the following instruments and equipment are required:

A nticollision light system—aviation red or white for small airplanes certificated after March 11, 1996

T achometer for each engine

O il pressure gauge for each engine

M anifold pressure gauge (for each altitude engine, i.e. turbocharged)

A ltimeter

T emperature gauge for each liquid-cooled engine

O il temperature gauge for each air-cooled engine

F uel gauge indicating the quantity in each tank

F lotation gear—if operated for hire over water beyond power-off gliding distance from shore

L anding gear position indicator, if the airplane has retractable gear

A irspeed indicator

M agnetic direction indicator

E mergency locator transmitter (if required by 14 CFR 91.207)

S afety belts (and shoulder harnesses for each front seat in aircraft manufactured after 1978)

19. **What instruments and equipment are required for VFR night flight?** (14 CFR 91.205)

For VFR flight at night, all the instruments and equipment for VFR day flight are required, plus the following:

F uses—one spare set or three fuses of each kind required accessible to the pilot in flight

L anding light—if the aircraft is operated for hire

A nticollision light system—approved aviation red or white

P osition lights—(navigation lights)

S ource of electrical energy—adequate for all installed electrical and radio equipment

20. **Who can perform maintenance on an aircraft?** (FAA-H-8083-25)

FAA-certificated A&P mechanic, an A&P mechanic with Inspector Authorization, an appropriately-rated FAA-certificated repair station, or the aircraft manufacturer.

21. **Define "preventive maintenance."** (FAA-H-8083-25, 14 CFR Part 43, AC 43-12)

Preventive maintenance means simple or minor preservation operations and the replacement of small standard parts not involving complex assembly operations. Certificated pilots, excluding student pilots, sport pilots, and recreational pilots, may perform preventive maintenance on any aircraft that is owned or operated by them provided that aircraft is not used in air carrier service. 14 CFR Part 43 Appendix A identifies typical preventive maintenance operations which include such basic items as oil changes, wheel bearing lubrication, hydraulic fluid (brakes, landing gear system) refills.

Exam Tip: Know where to look in the regulations for items approved for preventive maintenance: 14 CFR Part 43, Appendix A, Paragraph C—Preventive Maintenance.

22. What logbook entry information is required of the person performing preventive maintenance?
(FAA-H-8083-25, 14 CFR 43.3)

All pilots who maintain or perform preventive maintenance must make an entry in the maintenance record of the aircraft. The entry must include a description of the work, the date of completion of the work performed, and an entry of the pilot's name, signature, certificate number, and type of certificate held.

Additional Study Questions

1. During preflight, you discover that one of the position lights (installed equipment) is inoperative prior to a daytime flight. Can you legally conduct the flight? (14 CFR 91.213(d), FAA-H-8083-25)

2. How can a pilot determine if all applicable airworthiness directives have been complied with for his/her airplane? (FAA-H-8083-25, 14 CFR 91.417)

3. Explain how you will "deactivate" an item or system that has become inoperative in your airplane. Can you deactivate any item or system in the airplane? What is required? (FAA-H-8083-25, AC 91-67)

4. If the AFM for an aircraft you are about to fly is missing, what substitution may be made, if any? (14 CFR 91.9, FAA-H-8083-25)

5. Are the AFM Supplements required to be onboard the airplane? (FAA-H-8083-25)

6. As PIC, you have the responsibility for determining whether your aircraft is in a condition for safe flight. When flying rental aircraft, how can procedures regarding discrepancy records or "squawk" sheets, affect the total risk of a flight? (FAA Safety Briefing)

7. You have just completed the first leg of a long cross-country and notice that the oil level is approaching the one quart low mark. As a private pilot, can you add the quart of oil yourself or is a mechanic required? (14 CFR Part 43)

8. What are Special Airworthiness Safety Bulletins (SAIB)? Are they regulatory? (FAA-H-8083-25)

9. **During your preflight inspection, you discover that the left main tire on your aircraft has a large flat spot with nylon cord showing. You wisely decide that this is unacceptable and the tire should be replaced before flight. Do the regulations allow the pilot to perform this maintenance or must it be performed by a licensed mechanic (A&P)?** (14 CFR Part 43, Appendix A, Paragraph C – Preventive Maintenance)

10. **A 100-hour inspection was due at 3,302.5 hours. The 100 hour inspection was actually done at 3,309.5 hours. When is the next 100-hour inspection due?** (FAA-H-8083-25)

Weather
Information

3

A. Nature of the Atmosphere

1. State the general characteristics in regard to the flow of air around high and low pressure systems in the Northern Hemisphere. (AC 00-6)

Low Pressure—inward, upward, and counterclockwise

High Pressure— outward, downward, and clockwise

2. If your route of flight takes you towards a low-pressure system, in general, what kind of weather can you expect? What if you were flying towards a high-pressure system? (AC 00-6)

A low-pressure system is characterized by rising air, which is conducive to cloudiness, precipitation and bad weather. A high-pressure system is an area of descending air which tends to favor dissipation of cloudiness and good weather.

3. Describe the different types of fronts. (AC 00-6)

Cold front—occurs when a mass of cold, dense, and stable air advances and replaces a body of warmer air.

Occluded front—A frontal occlusion occurs when a fast-moving cold front catches up with a slow-moving warm front. Two types: cold front occlusion and warm front occlusion.

Warm front—The boundary area formed when a warm air mass contacts and flows over a colder air mass.

Stationery front—When the forces of two air masses are relatively equal, the boundary or front that separates them remains stationary and influences the local weather for days. The weather is typically a mixture of both warm and cold fronts.

4. **What are the general characteristics of the weather a pilot would encounter when operating near a cold front? A warm front?** (FAA-H-8083-25)

Cold Front—As the front passes, expected weather can include towering cumulus or cumulonimbus, heavy rain accompanied by lightning, thunder and/or hail; tornadoes possible; during passage, poor visibility, winds variable and gusting; temperature/dew point and barometric pressure drop rapidly.

Warm Front—As the front passes, expected weather can include stratiform clouds, drizzle, low ceilings and poor visibility; variable winds; rise in temperature.

Note: The weather associated with a front depends on the amount of moisture available, the degree of stability of the air that is forced upward, the slope of the front, the speed of frontal movement, and the upper wind flow.

5. **What is a "trough"?** (AC 00-6)

A trough (also called a trough line) is an elongated area of relatively low atmospheric pressure. At the surface when air converges into a low, it cannot go outward against the pressure gradient, nor can it go downward into the ground; it must go upward. Therefore, a low or trough is an area of rising air. Rising air is conducive to cloudiness and precipitation; hence the general association of low pressure and bad weather.

6. **What is a "ridge"?** (AC 00-6)

A ridge (also called a ridge line) is an elongated area of relatively high atmospheric pressure. Air moving out of a high or ridge depletes the quantity of air; therefore, these are areas of descending air. Descending air favors dissipation of cloudiness; hence the association of high pressure and good weather.

7. **What are the standard temperature and pressure values for sea level?** (AC 00-6)

15°C and 29.92" Hg

8. **What are "isobars"?** (AC 00-6)

An isobar is a line on a weather chart which connects areas of equal or constant barometric pressure.

9. If the isobars are relatively close together on a surface weather chart or a constant pressure chart, what information will this provide? (AC 00-6)

The spacing of isobars on these charts defines how steep or shallow a pressure gradient is. When isobars are spaced very close together, a steep pressure gradient exists which indicates higher wind speeds. A shallow pressure gradient (isobars not close together) usually means wind speeds will be less.

10. What causes the winds aloft to flow parallel to the isobars? (AC 00-6)

The Coriolis force.

11. Why do surface winds generally flow across the isobars at an angle? (AC 00-6)

Surface friction.

12. At what rate does atmospheric pressure decrease with an increase in altitude? (AC 00-6)

1" Hg per 1,000 feet.

13. What does "dew point" mean? (AC 00-6)

Dew point is the temperature to which a sample of air must be cooled to attain the state of saturation.

14. When temperature and dew point are close together (within 5°), what type of weather is likely? (AC 00-6)

Visible moisture in the form of clouds, dew, or fog. Also, these are ideal conditions for carburetor icing.

15. What factor primarily determines the type and vertical extent of clouds? (AC 00-6)

The stability of the atmosphere.

16. **Explain the difference between a stable atmosphere and an unstable atmosphere. Why is the stability of the atmosphere important?** (FAA-H-8083-25, AC 00-6)

    The stability of the atmosphere depends on its ability to resist vertical motion. A stable atmosphere makes vertical movement difficult, and small vertical disturbances dampen out and disappear. In an unstable atmosphere, small vertical air movements tend to become larger, resulting in turbulent airflow and convective activity. Instability can lead to significant turbulence, extensive vertical clouds, and severe weather.

17. **List the effects of stable and unstable air on clouds, turbulence, precipitation and visibility.** (AC 00-6)

	Stable	Unstable
Clouds	Stratiform	Cumuliform
Turbulence	Smooth	Rough
Precipitation	Steady	Showery
Visibility	Fair to Poor	Good

18. **When significant precipitation is occurring at the surface, how thick can you expect the clouds to be?** (AC 00-6)

    Significant precipitation usually requires clouds to be at least 4,000 feet thick. The heavier the precipitation, the thicker the clouds are likely to be.

19. **During your preflight planning, what type of meteorological information should you be aware of with respect to icing?** (AC 00-6)

    a. *Location of fronts* — A front's location, type, speed, and direction of movement.

    b. *Cloud layers* — The location of cloud bases and tops, which is valuable when determining if you will be able to climb above icing layers or descend beneath those layers into warmer air; reference PIREPs and area forecasts.

c. *Freezing level(s)* — Important when determining how to avoid icing and how to exit icing conditions if accidentally encountered.

d. *Air temperature and pressure* — Icing tends to be found in low-pressure areas and at temperatures at or around freezing.

20. What is the definition of the term freezing level and how can you determine where that level is? (AC 00-45)

The freezing level is the lowest altitude in the atmosphere over a given location at which the air temperature reaches 0°C. It is possible to have multiple freezing layers when a temperature inversion occurs above the defined freezing level. A pilot can use current icing products (CIP) and forecast icing products (FIP), as well as the freezing level graphics chart to determine the approximate freezing level. Other potential sources of icing information are: area forecasts, PIREPs, AIRMETs, SIGMETs, surface analysis charts, low-level significant weather charts, and winds and temperatures aloft (for air temperature at altitude).

21. What conditions are necessary for structural icing to occur? (AC 00-6)

Visible moisture and below freezing temperatures at the point moisture strikes the aircraft.

22. Name the main types of icing an aircraft may encounter in-flight. (AC 00-6)

Structural, induction system, and instrument icing.

23. Name the three types of structural icing that may occur in flight. (AC 00-6)

Clear ice — forms after initial impact when the remaining liquid portion of the drop flows out over the aircraft surface, gradually freezing as a smooth sheet of solid ice.

Rime ice — forms when drops are small, such as those in stratified clouds or light drizzle. The liquid portion remaining after initial impact freezes rapidly before the drop has time to spread out over aircraft surface.

Continued

Mixed ice—forms when drops vary in size or when liquid drops are intermingled with snow or ice particles. The ice particles become imbedded in clear ice, building a very rough accumulation.

24. What action is recommended if you inadvertently encounter icing conditions? (FAA-H-8083-15)

The first course of action should be to leave the area of visible moisture. This might mean descending to an altitude below the cloud bases, climbing to an altitude above the cloud tops, or turning to a different course.

25. Is frost considered to be hazardous to flight? Why? (AC 00-6)

Yes, because while frost does not change the basic aerodynamic shape of the wing, the roughness of its surface spoils the smooth flow of air, thus causing a slowing of airflow. This slowing of the air causes early airflow separation, resulting in a loss of lift. Even a small amount of frost on airfoils may prevent an aircraft from becoming airborne at normal takeoff speed. It is also possible that, once airborne, an aircraft could have insufficient margin of airspeed above stall so that moderate gusts or turning flight could produce incipient or complete stalling.

26. What factors must be present for a thunderstorm to form? (AC 00-6)

a. Sufficient water vapor

b. An unstable lapse rate

c. An initial upward boost (lifting) to start the storm process in motion

27. What are the three stages of a thunderstorm? (AC 00-6)

Cumulus stage—Updrafts cause raindrops to increase in size.

Mature stage—Rain at earth's surface; it falls through or immediately beside the updrafts; lightning; perhaps roll clouds.

Dissipating stage—Downdrafts and rain begin to dissipate.

28. What is a "temperature inversion"? (AC 00-6)

An inversion is an increase in temperature with height—a reversal of the normal decrease with height. An inversion aloft permits warm rain to fall through cold air below. Temperature in the cold air can be critical to icing. A ground-based inversion favors poor visibility by trapping fog, smoke, and other restrictions into low levels of the atmosphere. The air is stable, with little or no turbulence.

29. State two basic ways that fog may form. (AC 00-6)

a. Cooling air to the dew point.

b. Adding moisture to the air near the ground.

30. Name several types of fog. (AC 00-6)

a. Radiation fog

b. Advection fog

c. Upslope fog

d. Frontal fog or precipitation-induced fog

e. Steam fog

31. What causes radiation fog to form? (AC 00-6)

The ground cools the adjacent air to the dew point on calm, clear nights.

32. What is advection fog, and where is it most likely to form? (AC 00-6)

Advection fog results from the transport of warm humid air over a cold surface. A pilot can expect advection fog to form primarily along coastal areas during the winter. Unlike radiation fog, it may occur with winds, cloudy skies, over a wide geographic area, and at any time of the day or night.

33. What is upslope fog? (AC 00-6)

Upslope fog forms as a result of moist, stable air being cooled adiabatically as it moves up sloping terrain. Once the upslope wind ceases, the fog dissipates. Upslope fog is often quite dense and extends to high altitudes.

34. Define the term "wind shear," and state the areas in which it is likely to occur. (AC 00-6)

Wind shear is defined as the rate of change of wind velocity (direction and/or speed) per unit distance; conventionally expressed as vertical or horizontal wind shear. It may occur at any level in the atmosphere but three areas are of special concern:

a. Wind shear with a low-level temperature inversion.

b. Wind shear in a frontal zone or thunderstorm.

c. Clear air turbulence (CAT) at high levels associated with a jet stream or strong circulation.

35. Why is wind shear an operational concern to pilots? (AC 00-6)

Wind shear is an operational concern because unexpected changes in wind speed and direction can be potentially very hazardous to aircraft operations at low altitudes on approach to and departing from airports.

36. What types of weather information will you examine to determine if wind shear conditions might affect your flight? (AC 00-54)

a. *Terminal forecasts*—any mention of low level wind shear (LLWS) or the possibility of severe thunderstorms, heavy rain showers, hail, and wind gusts suggest the potential for LLWS and microbursts.

b. *METARs*—inspect for any indication of thunderstorms, rain showers, or blowing dust. Additional signs such as warming trends, gusty winds, cumulonimbus clouds, etc., should be noted.

c. *Severe weather watch reports, SIGMETS, and convective SIGMETS*—severe convective weather is a prime source for wind shear and microbursts.

d. *LLWAS (low level windshear alert system) reports*—installed at 110 airports in the U.S.; designed to detect wind shifts between outlying stations and a reference centerfield station.

e. *PIREPs*—reports of sudden airspeed changes on departure or approach and landing corridors provide a real-time indication of the presence of wind shear.

B. Obtaining Weather Information

1. What is the primary means of obtaining a weather briefing? (AIM 7-1-2, 7-1-4)

The flight service station (FSS) is the primary source for obtaining preflight briefings and inflight weather information. The FAA provides the Flight Service program through FSS's (both government and contract, 1-800-WX-BRIEF), and via the Internet, through Direct User Access Terminal System (DUATS), and Lockheed Martin Flight Services (DUATS II).

2. What are some examples of other sources of weather information? (AIM 7-1-2, 7-1-8)

a. Telephone Information Briefing Service, or TIBS (FSS).

b. Weather and aeronautical information available from numerous private industry sources.

c. DUATS and Lockheed Martin Flight Services via the internet. Pilots with a current medical certificate can receive preflight weather data and file domestic VFR and IFR flight plans.

d. In Alaska, Transcribed Weather Broadcast (TWEB and telephone access to the TWEB, or TEL-TWEB).

3. You're planning a cross-county flight. Does the weather data provided by commercial and/or third party vendors satisfy the preflight action required by 14 CFR 91.103? (AIM 7-1-3)

Pilots and operators should be aware that weather services provided by entities other than FAA, NWS or their contractors (such as the DUATS and Lockheed Martin Flight Services DUATS II) might not meet FAA/NWS quality control standards. All operators and pilots contemplating using such services should request and/or review an appropriate description of services and provider disclosure. When in doubt, consult with an FAA Flight Service Specialist.

4. What types of weather briefings are available from an AFSS/FSS briefer? (AIM 7-1-5)

Standard Briefing—Request when you are planning a flight and you have not received a previous briefing or have not received preliminary information through mass dissemination media (TIBS, TWEB in Alaska only, etc.).

Abbreviated Briefing—Request when you need information to supplement mass disseminated data, update a previous briefing, or when you need only one or two items.

Outlook Briefing—Request whenever your proposed time of departure is six or more hours from the time of the briefing; for planning purposes only.

Inflight Briefing—Request when needed to update a preflight briefing.

5. What pertinent information should a weather briefing include? (AIM 7-1-5)

a. Adverse Conditions

b. VFR Flight Not Recommended

c. Synopsis

d. Current Conditions

e. Enroute Forecast

f. Destination Forecast

g. Winds Aloft

h. Notices to Airmen (NOTAMs)

i. ATC Delay

j. Pilots may obtain the following from FSS briefers upon request: information on special use airspace (SUA) and SUA-related airspace, including alert areas, MOAs, MTRs (IFR, VFR, VR, and SR training routes), warning areas, and ATC assigned airspace (ATCAA); a review of the printed NOTAM publication; approximate density altitude data; information on air traffic services and rules; customs/immigration procedures; ADIZ rules; search and rescue; runway friction measurement value NOTAMs; GPS RAIM availability; and other assistance as required.

6. What is HIWAS? (AIM 7-1-10)

Hazardous In-flight Weather Advisory Service (HIWAS) is a continuous broadcast of in-flight weather advisories including summarized Aviation Weather Warnings, SIGMETs, Convective SIGMETs, Center Weather Advisories, AIRMETs, and urgent PIREPs. HIWAS is an additional source of hazardous weather information which makes this data available on a continuous basis. Navaids with HIWAS capability are depicted on sectional carts with an "H" in the upper right corner of the identification box. Where implemented, HIWAS alerts are broadcast on all except emergency frequencies once upon receipt by ARTCC, terminal facilities, and FSS.

7. What is a "flight information service" (FIS)? (FAA-H-8083-25)

Flight Information Service – Broadcast (FIS-B) is a ground broadcast service provided through the Automatic Dependent Surveillance – Broadcast (ADS-B) services network over the 978 MHz UAT data link. The FAA FIS-B system provides pilots and flight crews of properly-equipped aircraft with a flightdeck display of aviation weather and aeronautical information.

8. Can onboard datalink weather (FIS-B) be useful in navigating an aircraft safely around an area of thunderstorms? (AC 00-24; AIM 7-1-11)

Weather data linked from a ground weather surveillance radar system is not real-time information; it displays recent rather than current conditions. This data is typically updated every 5 minutes, but can be as much as 15 minutes old by the time it displays in the cockpit. Therefore, FIS aviation weather products are not appropriate for tactical avoidance of severe weather such as negotiating a path through a weather hazard area.

9. While en route, how can a pilot obtain updated weather information? (FAA-H-8083-25)

a. FSS on 122.2 and appropriate RCO (remote communication outlet) frequencies.

b. ATIS broadcasts along your route of flight.

c. HIWAS (Hazardous Inflight Weather Advisory Service).

d. Datalink weather—cockpit display of FIS-B information.

e. ATC (workload permitting).

C. Aviation Weather Reports and Observations

1. What is a METAR and what are the two types? (AC 00-45)

A METAR is an hourly surface observation of conditions observed at an airport. There are two types of METAR reports—a routine METAR report that is transmitted every hour and an aviation selected special weather report (SPECI). This is a special report that can be given at any time to update the METAR for rapidly changing weather conditions, aircraft mishaps, or other critical information.

2. Describe the basic elements of a METAR. (AC 00-45)

A METAR report contains the following elements in order as presented:

a. *Type of reports*—the METAR, and the SPECI (aviation special weather report).

b. *ICAO station identifier*—4-letter station identifiers; in the conterminous U.S., the 3-letter identifier is prefixed with K.

c. *Date and time of report*—a 6-digit date/time group appended with Z (UTC). First two digits are the date, then two for the hour, and two for minutes.

d. *Modifier (as required)*—if used, the modifier AUTO identifies the report as an automated weather report with no human intervention. If AUTO is shown in the body of the report, AO1 or AO2 will be encoded in the remarks section to indicate the type of precipitation sensor used at the station.

e. *Wind*—5-digit group (6 digits if speed is over 99 knots); first three digits = wind direction, in tens of degrees referenced to true north. Directions less than 100 degrees are preceded with a zero; next two digits are the average speed in knots, measured or estimated (or, if over 99 knots, the next three digits).

f. *Visibility*—surface visibility in statute miles, space, fractions of statute miles (as needed), and the letters SM.

g. *Runway visual range (RVR),* as required.

h. *Weather phenomena*—broken into two categories: qualifiers, and weather phenomena.

i. *Sky condition*—amount/height/type (as required) or indefinite ceiling/height (vertical visibility). Heights are recorded in feet AGL.

j. *Temperature/dew point group*—2-digit format in whole degrees Celsius, separated by a solidus (/). Temperatures below zero are prefixed with M.

k. *Altimeter*—4-digit format representing tens, units, tenths, and hundredths of inches of mercury prefixed with A. The decimal point is not reported or stated.

l. *Remarks (RMK), as required*—operational significant weather phenomena, location of phenomena, beginning and ending times, direction of movement.

Example: METAR KLAX 140651Z AUTO 00000KT 1SM
R35L/4500V6000FT -RA BR BKN030 10/10
A2990 RMK AO2

3. Describe several types of weather observing programs available. (AIM 7-1-12)

a. *Manual Observations*—with only a few exceptions, these reports are from airport locations staffed by FAA personnel who manually observe, perform calculations, and enter their observations into the communication system.

b. *AWOS*—Automated Weather Observing System; consists of various sensors, a processor, a computer-generated voice subsystem, and a transmitter to broadcast local, minute-by-minute weather data directly to the pilot. Observations will include the prefix AUTO in data.

Continued

c. *ASOS/AWSS*—Automated Surface Observing System/
Automated Weather Sensor System; the primary U.S. surface
weather observing systems. AWSS is a follow-on program
that provides the identical data as ASOS. Both systems provide continuous minute-by-minute observations that generate
METARs and other aviation weather information. Transmitted
over a discrete VHF radio frequency or the voice portion of a
local NAVAID, and are receivable to a maximum of 25 NM
from the station and a maximum altitude of 10,000 feet AGL.
Observations made without human intervention will include the
modifier "AUTO" in the report data.

4. What are PIREPs (UA), and where are they usually found? (AC 00-45)

A pilot report (PIREP) provides valuable information regarding the
conditions as they actually exist in the air, which cannot be gath-
ered from any other source. Pilots can confirm the height of bases
and tops of clouds, locations of wind shear and turbulence, and the
location of inflight icing. There are two types of PIREPs: routine or
"UA," and urgent or "UUA." PIREPs should be given to the ground
facility with which communications are established (i.e., FSS,
ARTCC, or terminal ATC). Altitudes are MSL, visibilities SM,
and distances in NM. PIREPs are available from an FSS and on the
internet via the ADDS web page at: **http://adds.aviationweather.
gov/pireps/**.

D. Aviation Weather Forecasts

1. What are Terminal Aerodrome Forecasts (TAFs)? (AC 00-45)

A terminal aerodrome forecast (TAF) is a concise statement of the
expected meteorological conditions significant to aviation for a
specified time period within five statute miles (SM) of the center of
the airport's runway complex (terminal). The TAFs use the same
weather codes found in METAR weather reports, in the following
format:

a. *Type of reports*—a routine forecast (TAF), an amended forecast
(TAF AMD), or a corrected forecast (TAF COR).

b. *ICAO station identifier*—4-letter station identifiers.

c. *Date and time of origin*—the date/time of forecast follows the terminal's location identifier. It contains the day of the month in two digits and time in four digits in which the forecast is completed and ready for transmission, with a Z appended to denote UTC. Example: 061737Z—the TAF was issued on the 6th day of the month at 1737 UTC.

d. *Valid period date and time*—The first two digits are the day of the month for the start of the TAF followed by two digits indicating the starting hour (UTC). The next two digits indicate the day of the month for the end of the TAF, and the last two digits are the ending hour (UTC) of the valid period. Scheduled 24- and 30-hour TAFs are issued four (4) times per day, at 0000, 0600, 1200, and 1800Z. Example: A 00Z TAF issued on the 9th of the month and valid for 24 hours would have a valid period of 0900/0924.

e. *Forecasts*—wind, visibility, significant and vicinity weather, cloud and vertical obscuration, non-convective low level wind shear, forecast change indicators (FM, TEMPO and PROB).

2. Define "aviation area forecast." (AC 00-45)

Abbreviated as "FA," this is a forecast of specified weather phenomena covering a flight information region or other area designated by the meteorological authority. Pilots should use the area forecast (in conjunction with AIRMETs, SIGMETs, convective SIGMETs, CWAs, etc.), to determine forecast en route weather and to interpolate conditions at airports that do not have a terminal aerodrome forecast (TAF). FAs are issued 3 times daily for each of the 6 areas in the contiguous 48 states. FAs are also issued for the Gulf of Mexico, the Caribbean, Hawaii, and Alaska. Most Areas Forecasts were canceled in 2017, replaced by GFAs.

3. What information is provided by an FA? (AC 00-45)

Area forecasts are issued for the conterminous U.S. and cover the airspace between the surface and 45,000 feet AMSL. They include:

a. *Synopsis*—brief discussion of the synoptic weather affecting the FA area during the 18-hour valid period.

Continued

b. *Clouds and weather*—description of the clouds and weather for the first 12-hour period for each state or group of states, including:

- Cloud amount (SCT, BKN or OVC) for clouds with bases higher than or equal to 1,000 feet AGL and below FL180,
- Cloud bases and tops (AMSL) associated with the above,
- Precipitation,
- Visibilities between 3 and 6 SM and obstruction(s) to visibility,
- Sustained surface winds 20 knots or greater.

c. *12 to 18-hour categorical outlook*—IFR, marginal VFR (MVFR), or VFR, including expected precipitation and/or obstruction(s) to visibility.

Note: Plans are to discontinue the six FAs covering the CONUS and one FA covering Hawaii, and subsequently replace them with digital and graphical products (GFA) produced by the NWS. No near-term changes are planned for the FAs for Alaska, the Caribbean, or the Gulf of Mexico.

4. What is a Graphical Forecast for Aviation (GFA)? (AWC)

The GFA is intended to provide the necessary aviation weather information as a complete picture of the weather that may impact flight in the continental U.S. The webpage includes observational data, forecasts, and warnings that can be viewed from 14 hours in the past to 15 hours in the future, including thunderstorms, clouds, flight category, precipitation, icing, turbulence and wind.

5. What are the four types of Inflight Aviation Weather Advisories? (AIM 7-1-5)

Inflight Aviation Weather Advisories are forecasts to advise enroute aircraft of the development of potentially hazardous weather in four types: the SIGMET (WS), the convective SIGMET (WST), the AIRMET (WA; text or graphical product), and the center weather advisory (CWA). All heights are referenced MSL, except in the case of ceilings (CIG) which indicate AGL.

6. What is a Convective SIGMET? (AC 00-45)

Convective SIGMETs (WST) implies severe or greater turbulence, severe icing and low-level wind shear. They may be issued for any convective situation which the forecaster feels is hazardous to all categories of aircraft. Convective SIGMET bulletins are issued for the Eastern (E), Central (C) and Western (W) United States (Convective SIGMETs are not issued for Alaska or Hawaii). Bulletins are issued hourly at H+55. Special bulletins are issued at any time as required and updated at H+55. The text of the bulletin consists of either an observation and a forecast, or just a forecast. The forecast is valid for up to 2 hours.

a. Severe thunderstorm due to:
 • Surface winds greater than or equal to 50 knots.
 • Hail at the surface greater than or equal to $3/4$ inches in diameter.
 • Tornadoes

b. Embedded thunderstorms

c. A line of thunderstorms

d. Thunderstorms producing greater than or equal to heavy precipitation that affects 40% or more of an area at least 3,000 square miles.

7. What is a SIGMET (WS)? (AIM 7-1-6)

A SIGMET (WS) advises of weather that is potentially hazardous to all aircraft. SIGMETs are unscheduled products that are valid for 4 hours; SIGMETs associated with tropical cyclones and volcanic ash clouds are valid for 6 hours. Unscheduled updates and corrections are issued as necessary. In the conterminous U.S., SIGMETs are issued when the following phenomena occur or are expected to occur:

a. Severe icing not associated with thunderstorms.

b. Severe or extreme turbulence or clear air turbulence (CAT) not associated with thunderstorms.

c. Widespread dust storms or sandstorms lowering surface visibilities to below 3 miles.

d. Volcanic ash.

8. What is an AIRMET (WA)? (AC 00-45)

Advisories of significant weather phenomena that describe conditions at intensities lower than those which require the issuance of SIGMETs, intended for use by *all* pilots in the preflight and enroute phase of flight to enhance safety. AIRMET information is available in two formats: text bulletins (WA) and graphics (G-AIRMET). They are issued on a scheduled basis every 6 hours beginning at 0245 UTC. Unscheduled updates and corrections are issued as necessary.

Each AIRMET Bulletin includes an outlook for conditions expected after the AIRMET valid period. AIRMETs contain details about IFR, extensive mountain obscuration, turbulence, strong surface winds, icing, and freezing levels.

9. What are the different types of AIRMETs? (AIM 7-1-6)

There are three AIRMET types: Sierra, Tango, and Zulu:

a. AIRMET Sierra describes IFR conditions and/or extensive mountain obscurations.

b. AIRMET Tango describes moderate turbulence, sustained surface winds of 30 knots or greater, and/or nonconvective low-level wind shear.

c. AIRMET Zulu describes moderate icing and provides freezing level heights.

10. Describe the winds and temperature aloft forecasts (FB). (AC 00-45)

Winds and temperature aloft forecasts are computer prepared forecasts of wind direction, wind speed, and temperature at specified times, altitudes, and locations. They are produced 4 times daily for specified locations in the continental United States, Hawaii, Alaska and coastal waters, and the western Pacific Ocean. Amendments are not issued to the forecasts. Wind forecasts are not issued for altitudes within 1,500 feet of a location's elevation.

Some of the features of FBs are:

a. Product header includes date and time observations collected, forecast valid date and time, and the time period during which the forecast is to be used.

b. Altitudes up to 15,000 feet referenced to MSL; altitudes at or above 18,000 feet are references to flight levels (FL).

c. Temperature indicated in degrees Celsius (two digits) for the levels from 6,000 through 24,000 feet. Above 24,000 feet, minus sign is omitted since temperatures are always negative at those altitudes. Temperature forecasts are not issued for altitudes within 2,500 feet of a location's elevation. Forecasts for intermediate levels are determined by interpolation.

d. Wind direction indicated in tens of degrees (two digits) with reference to true north and wind speed is given in knots (two digits). Light and variable wind or wind speeds of less than 5 knots are expressed by 9900. Forecast wind speeds of 100 through 199 knots are indicated by subtracting 100 from the speed and adding 50 to the coded direction. For example, a forecast of 250 degrees, 145 knots, is encoded as 7545. Forecast wind speeds of 200 knots or greater are indicated as a forecast speed of 199 knots. For example, 7799 is decoded as 270 degrees at 199 knots or greater.

11. What valuable information can be determined from Winds and Temperatures Aloft Forecasts (FB)?

Most favorable altitude—based on winds and direction of flight.

Areas of possible icing—by noting air temperatures of +2°C to -20°C.

Temperature inversions.

Turbulence—by observing abrupt changes in wind direction and speed at different altitudes.

12. What are Center Weather Advisories (CWA)? (AC 00-45)

A Center Weather Advisory (CWA) is an aviation warning for use by aircrews to anticipate and avoid adverse weather conditions in the en route and terminal environments. The CWA is not a flight planning product; instead it reflects current conditions expected at the time of issuance and/or is a short-range forecast for conditions expected to begin within 2 hours of issuance. CWAs are valid for a maximum of 2 hours. If conditions are expected to continue beyond the 2-hour valid period, a statement will be included in the CWA.

E. Aviation Weather Charts

1. Give some examples of the various NWS weather charts you will used during preflight planning. (AC 00-45)

a. Surface analysis chart

b. Weather depiction chart

c. Short-range surface prognostic chart

d. Significant weather prognostic chart

e. Convective outlook chart

f. Constant pressure analysis chart

2. What is a surface analysis chart? (AC 00-45)

Surface analysis charts are analyzed charts of surface weather observations. The chart depicts the distribution of several items including sea level pressure, the positions of highs, lows, ridges, troughs, the location and character of fronts, and the various boundaries such as drylines, outflow boundaries, sea-breeze fronts, and convergence lines. The chart is produced eight times daily.

3. What information does a weather depiction chart provide? (AC 00-45)

The weather depiction chart contains a plot of weather conditions at selected METAR stations and an analysis of weather flying category (VFR, MVFR, IFR). It is designed primarily as a briefing tool to alert aviation interests to the location of critical or near-critical operational minimums at terminals in the conterminous U.S. and surrounding land areas. The chart is issued eight times daily.

4. Define the terms: LIFR, IFR, MVFR and VFR. (AIM 7-1-7)

LIFR Low IFR—ceiling less than 500 feet and/or visibility less than 1 mile.

IFR Ceiling 500 to less than 1,000 feet and/or visibility 1 to less than 3 miles.

MVFR Marginal VFR—ceiling 1,000 to 3,000 feet and/or visibility 3 to 5 miles inclusive.

VFR Ceiling greater than 3,000 feet and visibility greater than 5 miles; includes sky clear.

5. What are short-range surface prognostic charts?
(AC 00-45)

Short-range surface prognostic (prog) charts provide a forecast of surface pressure systems, fronts and precipitation for a 2-1/2 day period. They cover a forecast area of the 48 contiguous states and coastal waters, and are prepared by the NWS Weather Prediction Center (and available on the AWC website). Predicted conditions are divided into five forecast periods: 12, 18, 24, 48 and 60 hours. Each chart depicts a snapshot of weather elements expected at the specified valid time. Charts are issued four times a day and can be used to obtain an overview of the progression of surface weather features during the included periods.

6. Describe a U.S. low-level significant weather prog chart.
(AC 00-45)

The low-level significant weather (SIGWX) charts provide a forecast of aviation weather hazards primarily intended to be used as guidance products for pre-flight briefings. The forecast domain covers the continental U.S. and the coastal waters for altitudes Flight Level 240 and below. Each depicts a "snapshot" of weather expected at the specified valid time. The charts depict weather flying categories, turbulence, and freezing levels, and are issued four times per day in two types: a 12-hour and a 24-hour prog.

7. Describe a mid-level significant weather (SIGWX) chart.
(AC 00-45)

The mid-level significant weather chart provides a forecast and an overview of significant en route weather phenomena over a range of flight levels from 10,000 feet MSL to FL450, and associated surface weather features. The chart is a "snapshot" of weather expected at the specified valid time and depicts numerous weather elements that can be hazardous to aviation. The AWC issues the 24-hour mid-level significant weather chart four times daily.

8. What is a convective outlook chart? (AC 00-45)

The convective outlook chart depicts areas forecast to have the potential for severe (tornado, wind gusts 50 knots or greater, or hail $\frac{3}{4}$ inch diameter size or greater) and non-severe (general) convec-

Continued

tion and specific severe weather threats during the following three days. The chart defines areas of slight risk (SLGT), moderate risk (MDT) or high risk (HIGH) of severe thunderstorms for a 24-hour period beginning at 1200 UTC. The Day 1 and Day 2 Convective Outlooks also depict areas of general thunderstorms (GEN TSTMS), while the Day 1, Day 2, and Day 3 Convective Outlooks may use SEE TEXT for areas where convection may approach or slightly exceed severe criteria.

9. What are constant pressure analysis charts? (AC 00-45)

Any surface of equal pressure in the atmosphere is a constant pressure surface. A constant pressure analysis chart is an upper air weather map where all information depicted is at the specified pressure of the chart. From these charts, a pilot can approximate the observed air temperature, wind, and temperature-dewpoint spread along a proposed route. They also depict highs, lows, troughs, and ridges aloft by the height contour patterns resembling isobars on a surface map. Twice daily, five constant pressure charts are issued from observed data obtained at 00Z and 12Z:

850 mb .... 5,000 ft
700 mb .... 10,000 ft
500 mb .... 18,000 ft
300 mb .... 30,000 ft
200 mb .... 39,000 ft

Exam Tip: Be prepared to interpret and discuss current and forecast weather along your planned route of flight. The evaluator will want you to demonstrate that you can interpret the various aviation weather reports, forecasts, charts/graphics and make an assessment of how it will affect your planned flight.

Additional Study Questions

1. When evaluating the weather reports and forecasts during your pre-flight planning, what process will you use to make a go/no-go decision? (FAA-H-8083-25)

2. Decode the following pilot weather report (PIREP): (AIM 7-1-20)

   KCMH UA/OV KAPE 230010/TM 1516/FL085/TP BE20/SK BKN 065/WX FV03SM HZ FU/TA 20/TB LGT

3. Decode the following METAR and Terminal Aerodrome Forecast (TAF): (AIM 7-1-30)

   METAR KPIT 091955Z COR 22015G25KT 3/4SM R28L/2600FT TSRA OVC010CB 18/16 A2992 RMK SLP045 T01820159

   TAF KPIT 091730Z 0918/1024 15005KT 5SM HZ FEW020 WS010/31022KT

   FM091930 30015G25KT 3SM SHRA OVC015

   TEMPO 0920/0922 1/2SM +TSRA OVC008CB

   FM100100 27008KT 5SM SHRA BKN020 OVC040

   PROB30 1004/1007 1SM RA BR

   FM101015 18005KT 6SM SHRA OVC020

   BECMG 1013/1015 P6SM NSW SKC

4. What symbols are used to depict the following frontal systems on surface analysis charts? Cold, Warm, Stationary, Occluded. (AC 00-6)

5. What is a microburst? When and where are they most likely to occur? (AIM 7-1-26)

6. What is a sea breeze, and why does it occur? (AC 00-6)

7. What is a mountain wave? (AC 00-6)

8. Define the term "ceiling." (AC 00-6)

9. **Give some examples of charts and reports useful in determining the potential for and location of thunderstorms along your route.** (AC 00-45)

10. **If your destination has no Terminal Forecast, which primary source of information should be referenced for forecasted weather at the estimated time of arrival?** (AC 00-45)

11. **How can a pilot reduce or eliminate the risks associated with flying in a constantly changing weather environment?** (FAA-H-8083-25)

12. **One way to control risk is to set personal minimums. What personal weather minimums would you establish for yourself?** (FAA-H-8083-2)

13. **When considering the possibility that the weather may be different than what was forecast, what can you do before departure and while en route to reduce the overall risk?** (FAA-H-8083-2)

Performance
and Limitations

4

A. Aerodynamics

1. What are the four dynamic forces that act on an airplane during all maneuvers? (FAA-H-8083-25)

Lift—the upward acting force

Gravity—or weight, the downward acting force

Thrust—the forward acting force

Drag—the backward acting force

2. What flight condition will result in the sum of the opposing forces being equal? (FAA-H-8083-25)

In steady-state, straight-and-level, unaccelerated flight, the sum of the opposing forces is equal to zero. There can be no unbalanced forces in steady, straight flight (Newton's Third Law). This is true whether flying level or when climbing or descending. It does not mean the four forces are equal. It means the opposing forces are equal to, and thereby cancel the effects of each other.

3. What is an airfoil? State some examples. (FAA-H-8083-25)

An airfoil is a device which gets a useful reaction from air moving over its surface, namely LIFT. Wings, horizontal tail surfaces, vertical tail surfaces, and propellers are examples of airfoils.

4. What is the "angle of incidence"? (FAA-H-8083-25)

The angle of incidence is the angle formed by the longitudinal axis of the airplane and the chord of the wing. It is measured by the angle at which the wing is attached to the fuselage. The angle of incidence is fixed and cannot be changed by the pilot.

5. What is a "relative wind"? (FAA-H-8083-25)

The relative wind is the direction of the airflow with respect to the wing. When a wing is moving forward and downward the relative wind moves backward and upward. The flight path and relative wind are always parallel but travel in opposite directions.

6. What is the "angle of attack"? (FAA-H-8083-25)

The angle of attack is the angle between the wing chord line and the direction of the relative wind; it can be changed by the pilot.

7. What is "Bernoulli's Principle"? (FAA-H-8083-25)

Bernoulli's Principle—The pressure of a fluid (liquid or gas) decreases at points where the speed of the fluid increases. In the case of airflow, high speed flow is associated with low pressure and low speed flow with high pressure. The airfoil of an aircraft is designed to increase the velocity of the airflow above its surface, thereby decreasing pressure above the airfoil. Simultaneously, the impact of the air on the lower surface of the airfoil increases the pressure below. This combination of pressure decrease above and increase below produces lift.

8. What are several factors which will affect both lift and drag?

Wing area—Lift and drag acting on a wing are roughly proportional to the wing area. A pilot can change wing area by using certain types of flaps (i.e., Fowler flaps).

Shape of the airfoil—As the upper curvature of an airfoil is increased (up to a certain point) the lift produced increases. Lowering an aileron or flap device can accomplish this. Also, ice or frost on a wing can disturb normal airflow, changing its camber, and disrupting its lifting capability.

Angle of attack—As angle of attack is increased, both lift and drag are increased, up to a certain point.

Velocity of the air—An increase in velocity of air passing over the wing increases lift and drag.

Air density—Lift and drag vary directly with the density of the air. As air density increases, lift and drag increase. As air density decreases, lift and drag decrease. Air density is affected by these factors: pressure, temperature, and humidity.

9. What is "torque effect"? (FAA-H-8083-25)

Torque effect involves Newton's Third Law of Physics — for every action, there is an equal and opposite reaction. Applied to the airplane, this means that as the internal engine parts and the propeller are revolving in one direction, an equal force is trying to rotate the airplane in the opposite direction. It is greatest when at low airspeeds with high power settings and a high angle of attack.

10. What effect does torque reaction have on an airplane on the ground and in flight? (FAA-H-8083-25)

In flight — torque reaction is acting around the longitudinal axis, tending to make the airplane roll. To compensate, some of the older airplanes are rigged in a manner to create more lift on the wing that is being forced downward. The more modern airplanes are designed with the engine offset to counteract this effect of torque.

On the ground — during the takeoff roll, an additional turning moment around the vertical axis is induced by torque reaction. As the left side of the airplane is being forced down by torque reaction, more weight is being placed on the left main landing gear. This results in more ground friction, or drag, on the left tire than on the right, causing a further turning moment to the left.

11. What are the four factors that contribute to torque effect? (FAA-H-8083-25)

Torque reaction of the engine and propeller. For every action there is an equal and opposite reaction. The rotation of the propeller (from the cockpit) to the right, tends to roll or bank the airplane to the left.

Gyroscopic effect of the propeller. Gyroscopic precession applies here: the resultant action or deflection of a spinning object when a force is applied to the outer rim of its rotational mass. If the axis of a propeller is tilted, the resulting force will be exerted 90° ahead in the direction of rotation and in the same direction as the applied force. It is most noticeable on takeoffs in taildraggers when the tail is raised.

Continued

Corkscrewing effect of the propeller slipstream. High-speed rotation of an airplane propeller results in a corkscrewing rotation to the slipstream as it moves rearward. At high propeller speeds and low forward speeds (as in a takeoff), the slipstream strikes the vertical tail surface on the left side pushing the tail to the right and yawing the airplane to the left.

Asymmetrical loading of the propeller (P-Factor). When an airplane is flying with a high angle of attack, the bite of the downward moving propeller blade is greater than the bite of the upward moving blade. This is due to the downward moving blade meeting the oncoming relative wind at a greater angle of attack than the upward moving blade. Consequently there is greater thrust on the downward moving blade on the right side, and this forces the airplane to yaw to the left.

12. What is "centrifugal force"? (FAA-H-8083-25)

Centrifugal force is the "equal and opposite reaction" of the airplane to the change in direction, and it acts "equal and opposite" to the horizontal component of lift.

13. What is "load factor"? (FAA-H-8083-25)

Load factor is the ratio of the total load supported by the airplane's wing to the actual weight of the airplane and its contents. In other words, it is the actual load supported by the wings divided by the total weight of the airplane. It can also be expressed as the ratio of a given load to the pull of gravity; i.e., to refer to a load factor of three as "3 Gs." In this case the weight of the airplane is equal to 1 G, and if a load of three times the actual weight of the airplane were imposed upon the wing due to curved flight, the load factor would be equal to 3 Gs.

14. For what two reasons is load factor important to pilots? (FAA-H-8083-25)

a. Because of the obviously dangerous overload that it is possible for a pilot to impose on the aircraft structure.

b. Because an increased load factor increases the stalling speed and makes stalls possible at seemingly safe flight speeds.

15. What situations may result in load factors reaching the maximum or being exceeded? (FAA-H-8083-25)

Level Turns — The load factor increases at a terrific rate after a bank has reached 45° or 50°. The load factor in a 60°-bank turn is 2 Gs. The load factor in a 80°-bank turn is 5.76 Gs. The wing must produce lift equal to these load factors if altitude is to be maintained.

Turbulence — Severe vertical gusts cause a sudden increase in angle of attack, resulting in large loads which are resisted by the inertia of the airplane.

Speed — The amount of excess load that can be imposed upon the wing depends on how fast the airplane is flying. At speeds below maneuvering speed, the airplane will stall before the load factor can become excessive. At speeds above maneuvering speed, the limit load factor for which an airplane is stressed can be exceeded by abrupt or excessive application of the controls or by strong turbulence.

16. What are the different operational categories for aircraft and within which category does your aircraft fall? (FAA-H-8083-25)

The maximum safe load factors (limit load factors) specified for airplanes in the various categories are as follows:

Normal .... +3.8 to -1.52

Utility (mild aerobatics including spins) .... +4.4 to -1.76

Aerobatic .... +6.0 to -3.00

17. What effect does an increase in load factor have on stalling speed? (FAA-H-8083-25)

As load factor increases, stalling speed increases. Any airplane can be stalled at any airspeed within the limits of its structure and the strength of the pilot. At a given airspeed the load factor increases as angle of attack increases, and the wing stalls because the angle of attack has been increased to a certain angle. Therefore, there is a direct relationship between the load factor imposed upon the wing and its stalling characteristics. A rule for determining the speed at which a wing will stall is that the stalling speed increases in proportion to the square root of the load factor.

18. **Define the term "maneuvering speed."** (FAA-H-8083-25, SAIB CE-11-17)

Maneuvering speed is the maximum speed at which the limit load can be imposed (either by gusts or full deflection of the control surfaces) without causing structural damage. It is the speed below which you can, in smooth air, move a single flight control one time, to its full deflection, for one axis of airplane rotation only (pitch, roll or yaw) without risk of damage to the airplane. Speeds up to, but not exceeding the maneuvering speed allow an aircraft to stall prior to experiencing an increase in load factor that would exceed the limit load of the aircraft.

Note: Operating at or below maneuvering speed does not provide structural protection against multiple full control inputs in one axis or full control inputs in more than one axis at the same time.

19. **Discuss the effect on maneuvering speed of an increase or decrease in weight.** (FAA-H-8083-25)

Maneuvering speed increases with an increase in weight and decreases with a decrease in weight. An aircraft operating at a reduced weight is more vulnerable to rapid accelerations encountered during flight through turbulence or gusts. Design limit load factors could be exceeded if a reduction in maneuvering speed is not accomplished. An aircraft operating at or near gross weight in turbulent air is much less likely to exceed design limit load factors and may be operated at the published maneuvering speed for gross weight if necessary.

20. **Define "loss-of-control-inflight" (LOC-I) and describe several situations that might increase the risk of an LOC-I accident occurring.** (FAA-H-8083-3)

LOC-I is defined as a significant deviation of an aircraft from the intended flight path and it often results from an airplane upset. Maneuvering is the most common phase of flight for LOC-I accidents to occur; however, LOC-I accidents occur in all phases of flight. Situations that increase the risk of this include uncoordinated flight, equipment malfunctions, pilot complacency, distraction, turbulence, and poor risk management, such as attempting to fly in IMC when the pilot is not qualified or proficient in it.

21. What causes an airplane to stall? (FAA-H-8083-25)

The direct cause of every stall is an excessive angle of attack. Each airplane has a particular angle of attack where the airflow separates from the upper surface of the wing and the stall occurs. This critical angle of attack varies from 16° to 20° depending on the airplane's design, but each airplane has only one specific angle of attack where the stall occurs, regardless of airspeed, weight, load factor, or density altitude.

22. What is a "spin"? (AC 61-67)

A spin in a small airplane or glider is a controlled (recoverable) or uncontrolled (possibly unrecoverable) maneuver in which the airplane or glider descends in a helical path while flying at an angle of attack greater than the critical angle of attack. Spins result from aggravated stalls in either a slip or a skid. If a stall does not occur, a spin cannot occur.

23. What causes a spin? (AC 61-67)

The primary cause of an inadvertent spin is exceeding the critical angle of attack while applying excessive or insufficient rudder, and to a lesser extent, aileron.

24. When are spins most likely to occur? (AC 61-67)

A stall/spin situation can occur in any phase of flight but is most likely to occur in the following situations:

a. *Engine failure on takeoff during climbout*—pilot tries to stretch glide to landing area by increasing back pressure or makes an uncoordinated turn back to departure runway at a relatively low airspeed.

b. *Crossed-control turn from base to final (slipping or skidding turn)*—pilot overshoots final (possibly due to a crosswind) and makes uncoordinated turn at a low airspeed.

c. *Engine failure on approach to landing*—pilot tries to stretch glide to runway by increasing back pressure.

d. *Go-around with full nose-up trim*—pilot applies power with full flaps and nose-up trim combined with uncoordinated use of rudder.

Continued

e. *Go-around with improper flap retraction*—pilot applies power and retracts flaps rapidly resulting in a rapid sink rate followed by an instinctive increase in back pressure.

25. What procedure should be used to recover from an inadvertent spin? (AC 61-67)

a. Close the throttle (if not already accomplished).

b. Neutralize the ailerons.

c. Apply full opposite rudder.

d. Briskly move the elevator control forward to approximately the neutral position. (Some aircraft require merely a relaxation of back pressure; others require full forward elevator pressure).

e. Once the stall is broken the spinning will stop. Neutralize the rudder when the spinning stops.

f. When the rudder is neutralized, gradually apply enough aft elevator pressure to return to level flight.

Remember: P A R E

P ower—reduce to idle

A ilerons—position to neutral

R udder—apply full opposite against rotation

E levator—apply positive, forward of neutral, movement to break stall

Once the spin rotation stops, neutralize the rudder and begin applying back pressure to return to level flight.

26. What causes "adverse yaw"? (FAA-H-8083-25)

When turning an airplane to the left for example, the downward deflected aileron on the right produces more lift on the right wing. Since the downward deflected right aileron produces more lift, it also produces more drag, while the opposite left aileron has less lift and less drag. This added drag attempts to pull or veer the airplane's nose in the direction of the raised wing (right); that is, it tries to turn the airplane in the direction opposite to that desired. This undesired veering is referred to as adverse yaw.

27. What is "ground effect"? (FAA-H-8083-3)

Ground effect is a condition of improved performance the airplane experiences when it is operating near the ground. A change occurs in the three-dimensional flow pattern around the airplane because the airflow around the wing is restricted by the ground surface. This reduces the wing's upwash, downwash, and wingtip vortices. In order for ground effect to be of a significant magnitude, the wing must be quite close to the ground.

28. What major problems can be caused by ground effect? (FAA-H-8083-3)

During landing, at a height of approximately one-tenth of a wing span above the surface, drag may be 40 percent less than when the airplane is operating out of ground effect. Therefore, any excess speed during the landing phase may result in a significant float distance. In such cases, if care is not exercised by the pilot, he/she may run out of runway and options at the same time.

During takeoff, due to the reduced drag in ground effect, the aircraft may seem capable of takeoff well below the recommended speed. However, as the airplane rises out of ground effect with a deficiency of speed, the greater induced drag may result in very marginal climb performance, or the inability of the airplane to fly at all. In extreme conditions, such as high temperature, high gross weight, and high-density altitude, the airplane may become airborne initially with a deficiency of speed and then settle back to the runway.

B. Weight and Balance

1. Define the following: (FAA-H-8083-1; FAA-H-8083-25)

Empty weight—The weight of the airframe, engines, all permanently installed equipment, and unusable fuel. Depending on the FARs under which the aircraft was certificated, either the undrainable oil or full reservoir of oil is included.

Gross weight—The maximum allowable weight of both the airplane and its contents.

Continued

Useful load—The weight of the pilot, copilot, passengers, baggage, usable fuel and drainable oil.

Arm—The horizontal distance in inches from the reference datum line to the center of gravity of the item.

Moment—The product of the weight of an item multiplied by its arm. Moments are expressed in pound-inches.

Center of gravity—The point about which an aircraft would balance if it were possible to suspend it at that point. Expressed in inches from datum.

Datum—An imaginary vertical plane or line from which all measurements of arm are taken. Established by the manufacturer.

2. **What basic equation is used in all weight and balance problems to find the center of gravity location of an airplane and/or its components?** (FAA-H-8083-25)

Weight x Arm = Moment

By rearrangement of this equation to the forms:

Weight = Moment ÷ Arm

$$\text{Arm (CG)} = \frac{\text{(Total) Moment}}{\text{(Total) Weight}}$$

With any two known values, the third value can be found.

Remember: W A M
(Weight x Arm = Moment)

3. **What performance characteristics will be adversely affected when an aircraft has been overloaded?**
   (FAA-H-8083-1)

   a. Higher takeoff speed

   b. Longer takeoff run

   c. Reduced rate and angle of climb

   d. Lower maximum altitude

   e. Shorter range

   f. Reduced cruising speed

   g. Reduced maneuverability

   h. Higher stalling speed

   i. Higher landing speed

   j. Longer landing roll

   k. Excessive weight on the nosewheel

4. What effect does a forward center of gravity have on an aircraft's flight characteristics? (FAA-H-8083-1)

Higher stall speed—stalling angle of attack is reached at a higher speed due to increased wing loading.

Slower cruise speed—increased drag; greater angle of attack is required to maintain altitude.

More stable—the center of gravity is farther forward from the center of pressure which increases longitudinal stability.

Greater back elevator pressure required—longer takeoff roll; higher approach speeds and problems with landing flare.

5. What effect does a rearward center of gravity have on an aircraft's flight characteristics? (FAA-H-8083-1)

Lower stall speed—less wing loading.

Higher cruise speed—reduced drag; smaller angle of attack is required to maintain altitude.

Less stable—stall and spin recovery more difficult; the center of gravity is closer to the center of pressure, causing longitudinal instability.

6. What are the standard weights assumed for the following when calculating weight and balance problems? (FAA-H-8083-25, AC 120-27)

Crew and passengers .... 190 lbs each
Gasoline .... 6 lbs/U.S. gal
Oil .... 7.5 lbs/U.S. gal
Water .... 8.35 lbs/U.S. gal

C. Aircraft Performance

1. **What are some of the main elements of aircraft performance?** (FAA-H-8083-25)

   a. Takeoff and landing distance

   b. Rate of climb

   c. Ceiling

   d. Payload

   e. Range

   f. Speed

   g. Fuel economy

   h. Maneuverability

   i. Stability

2. **What factors affect the performance of an aircraft during takeoffs and landings?** (FAA-H-8083-25)

   a. Air density (density altitude)

   b. Surface wind

   c. Runway surface

   d. Upslope or downslope of runway

   e. Weight

3. **What effect does wind have on aircraft performance?** (FAA-H-8083-25)

   Takeoff—The effect of a headwind is to allow the aircraft to reach the lift-off speed at a lower ground speed, which will increase airplane performance by shortening the takeoff distance and increasing the angle of climb. The effect of a tailwind is the aircraft needs to achieve greater ground speed to get to lift-off speed. This decreases aircraft performance by increasing takeoff distance and reducing the angle of climb.

Landing—The effect of wind on landing distance is identical to its effect on takeoff distance. A headwind will lower ground speed and increase airplane performance by steepening the approach angle and reducing the landing distance. A tailwind will increase ground speed and decrease performance, by decreasing the approach angle and increasing the landing distance.

Cruise flight—Winds aloft have somewhat an opposite effect on airplane performance. A headwind will decrease performance by reducing ground speed, which in turn increases the fuel requirement for the flight. A tailwind will increase performance by increasing the ground speed, which in turn reduces the fuel requirement for the flight.

4. How does weight affect takeoff and landing performance? (FAA-H-8083-25)

Increased gross weight can have a significant effect on takeoff performance:

a. Higher liftoff speed;

b. Greater mass to accelerate (slow acceleration);

c. Increased retarding force (drag and ground friction); and

d. Longer takeoff distance.

The effect of gross weight on landing distance is that the airplane will require a greater speed to support the airplane at the landing angle of attack and lift coefficient resulting in an increased landing distance.

5. What effect does an increase in density altitude have on takeoff and landing performance? (FAA-P-8740-2)

An increase in density altitude results in:

a. Increased takeoff distance (greater takeoff TAS required).

b. Reduced rate of climb (decreased thrust and reduced acceleration)

c. Increased true airspeed on approach and landing (same IAS).

d. Increased landing roll distance.

6. Define the term "density altitude." (FAA-H-8083-25)

Density altitude is pressure altitude corrected for nonstandard temperature. Under standard atmospheric condition, air at each level in the atmosphere has a specific density, and under standard conditions, pressure altitude and density altitude identify the same level. Therefore, density altitude is the vertical distance above sea level in the standard atmosphere at which a given density is found.

7. How does air density affect aircraft performance? (FAA-H-8083-25)

The density of the air has a direct effect on:

a. Lift produced by the wings;

b. Power output of the engine;

c. Propeller efficiency; and

d. Drag forces

8. What factors affect air density? (FAA-P-8740-2)

Altitude—the higher the altitude, the less dense the air.

Temperature—the warmer the air, the less dense it is.

Humidity—more humid air is less dense.

9. How does temperature, altitude, and humidity affect density altitude? (FAA-P-8740-2)

a. Density altitude will increase (low air density) when one or more of the following occurs:
   - High air temperature
   - High altitude
   - High humidity

b. Density altitude will decrease (high air density) when one or more of the following occurs:
   - Low air temperature
   - Low altitude
   - Low humidity

10. Know the following speeds for your airplane!

V_{S0}—Stall speed in landing configuration; the calibrated power-off stalling speed or the minimum steady flight speed at which the airplane is controllable in the landing configuration.

V_{S1}—Stall speed clean or in specified configuration; the calibrated power-off stalling speed or the minimum steady flight speed at which the airplane is controllable in a specified configuration.

V_Y—Best rate-of-climb speed; the calibrated airspeed at which the airplane will obtain the maximum increase in altitude per unit of time. This best rate-of-climb speed normally decreases slightly with altitude.

V_X—Best angle-of-climb speed; the calibrated airspeed at which the airplane will obtain the highest altitude in a given horizontal distance. This best angle-of-climb speed normally increases with altitude.

V_{LE}—Maximum landing gear extension speed; the maximum calibrated airspeed at which the airplane can be safely flown with the landing gear extended. This is a problem involving stability and controllability.

V_{LO}—Maximum landing gear operating speed; the maximum calibrated airspeed at which the landing gear can be safely extended or retracted. This is a problem involving the airloads imposed on the operating mechanism during extension or retraction of the gear.

V_{FE}—Maximum flap extension speed; the highest calibrated airspeed permissible with the wing flaps in a prescribed extended position. This is a problem involving the airloads imposed on the structure of the flaps.

V_A—Maneuvering speed; the calibrated design maneuvering airspeed. This is the maximum speed at which the limit load can be imposed (either by gusts or full deflection of the control surfaces) without causing structural damage.

V_{NO}—Normal operating speed; the maximum calibrated airspeed for normal operation or the maximum structural cruise speed. This is the speed above which exceeding the limit load factor may cause permanent deformation of the airplane structure.

V_{NE}—Never exceed speed; the calibrated airspeed which should never be exceeded. If flight is attempted above this speed, structural damage or structural failure may result.

11. **What information can you obtain from the following charts?** (FAA-H-8083-25)

    a. *Takeoff charts*—These allow you to compute the takeoff distance of the airplane with no flaps or with a specific flap configuration. You can also compute distances for a no flap takeoff over a 50-foot obstacle scenario as well as with flaps over a 50-foot obstacle. The takeoff distance chart provides for various airplane weights, altitudes, temperatures, winds, and obstacle heights.

    b. *Fuel, time, and distance-to-climb chart*—This chart will give the fuel amount used during the climb, the time it will take to accomplish the climb, and the ground distance that will be covered during the climb. To use this chart, obtain the information for the departing airport and for the cruise altitude.

    c. *Cruise and range performance chart*—This is designed to give true airspeed, fuel consumption, endurance in hours, and range in miles at specific cruise configurations.

    d. *Crosswind and headwind component chart*—This allows for figuring the headwind and crosswind component for any given wind direction and velocity.

    e. *Landing charts*—Provide normal landing distance as well as landing distance over a 50-foot obstacle.

    f. *Stall speed performance charts*—These are designed to give an understanding of the speed at which the airplane will stall in a given configuration. Will typically take into account the angle of bank, the position of the gear and flaps, and the throttle position.

12. **Define the term "pressure altitude," and state why it is important.** (FAA-H-8083-3)

    Pressure Altitude—the altitude indicated when the altimeter setting window (barometric scale) is adjusted to 29.92. This is the altitude above the standard datum plane, a theoretical plane where air pressure (corrected to 15°C) equals 29.92 in. Hg. Pressure altitude is used to compute density altitude, true altitude, true airspeed, and other performance data.

13. **The following questions are designed to provide pilots with a general review of the basic information they should know about their specific airplane before taking a flight check or review.**

What is the normal climb-out speed? _____

What is the best rate-of-climb speed? _____

What is the best angle-of-climb speed? _____

What is the maximum flap extension speed? _____

What is the maximum gear extension speed? _____

What is the stall speed in the normal landing configuration?

_____

What is the stall speed in the clean configuration? _____

What is the normal approach-to-land speed? _____

What is maneuvering speed? _____

What is red-line speed? _____

What engine-out glide speed will give you maximum range?

_____

What is the make and horsepower of the engine?

_____ _____

How many usable gallons of fuel can you carry? _____

Where are the fuel tanks located, and what are their capacities?

_____ _____

Where are the fuel vents for your aircraft?

_____

What is the octane rating of the fuel used by your aircraft?

_____

Where are the fuel sumps located on your aircraft? When should you drain them?

_____

What are the minimum and maximum oil capacities?

_____ _____

Continued

What weight of oil is being used? _____

What is the maximum oil temperature and pressure?

_____ _____

Is the landing gear fixed, manual, hydraulic or electric? If retractable, what is the backup system for lowering the gear?

_____ _____

What are the nosewheel turning limitations for your aircraft?

_____

What is the maximum allowable/demonstrated crosswind component for the aircraft? _____

How many people will this aircraft carry safely with a full fuel load? _____

What is the maximum allowable weight the aircraft can carry with baggage in the baggage compartment? _____

What takeoff distance is required if a takeoff were made from a sea-level pressure altitude? _____

What is your maximum allowable useful load? _____

Solve a weight and balance problem for the flight you plan to make with one passenger at 170 pounds.

a. Does your load fall within the weight and balance envelope?

_____

b. What is the final gross weight? _____

c. How much fuel can be carried? _____

d. How much baggage can be carried with full fuel? _____

e. Know the function of the various types of antennae on your aircraft. _____

Additional Study Questions

1. You have just landed on a 2,100-foot grass strip to pick up two passengers and you plan to depart in the early afternoon. The temperature will be warmer than expected, so you compute the density altitude and determine that the required takeoff distance over a 50-foot obstacle will be 2,000 feet. Your weight and balance calculation indicates you will be 100 pounds under gross weight. If you decide to takeoff, explain the potential hazards, the overall risk, and the actions you could take to mitigate that risk. (FAA-H-8083-2)

2. Why are some aircraft not allowed to perform forward slips with flaps extended? (AFM)

3. While enroute, will the CG change as your aircraft uses fuel? (FAA-H-8083-25)

4. What causes an airplane (except a T-tail) to pitch nosedown when power is reduced and controls are not adjusted? (FAA-H-8083-25)

5. Will the indicated airspeed at which an aircraft stalls change as altitude is increased? (FAA-H-8083-25)

6. How does an aircraft's limitations (performance, fuel capacity, navigation capability) affect the total risk of a flight? What can a pilot do to mitigate that risk? (FAA-H-8083-2)

7. What force causes an airplane to turn? (FAA-H-8083-25)

8. The amount of excess load that can be imposed on the structure of an airplane is dependent on what factor? (FAA-H-8083-25)

9. Define the terms "service ceiling" and "absolute ceiling." What are their values for your aircraft? (FAA-H-8083-25)

10. The performance chart numbers for your aircraft are based on test flights conducted in a new aircraft. During preflight planning, how can a pilot minimize risk when using the charts to make performance calculations for takeoff, enroute cruise, and landing? (FAA-H-8083-25)

11. You're planning a VFR departure from Durango Colorado KDRO (elevation 6,689 feet MSL) in a Cessna 172. Explain the potential hazards that exist when departing KDRO as compared to departing KLAX (elevation 127 feet MSL). Is there anything you can do to mitigate the risk? (FAA-H-8083-2)

Operation of Systems

5

Some of the following questions reference the systems of a Cessna 152. Be sure to review your aircraft's AFM or POH.

A. Aircraft and Engine Operations

1. What are the four main control surfaces and what are their functions? (FAA-H-8083-25)

Elevators—The elevators control the movement of the airplane about its lateral axis. This motion is called pitch.

Ailerons—The ailerons control the airplane's movement about its longitudinal axis. This motion is called roll.

Rudder—The rudder controls movement of the airplane about its vertical axis. This motion is called yaw.

Trim Tabs—Trim tabs are small, adjustable hinged-surfaces on the aileron, rudder, or elevator control surfaces. They are labor-saving devices that enable the pilot to release manual pressure on the primary control.

2. How are the various flight controls operated? (AFM)

The flight control surfaces are manually actuated through use of either a rod or cable system. A control wheel actuates the ailerons and elevator, and rudder/brake pedals actuate the rudder.

3. What are flaps and what is their function? (FAA-H-8083-25)

The wing flaps are movable panels on the inboard trailing edges of the wings. They are hinged so that they may be extended downward into the flow of air beneath the wings to increase both lift and drag. Their purpose is to permit a slower airspeed and a steeper angle of descent during a landing approach. In some cases, they may also be used to shorten the takeoff distance.

4. Describe the landing gear system on this airplane. (AFM)

The landing gear consists of a tricycle-type system utilizing two main wheels and a steerable nosewheel. Tubular spring steel main gear struts provide main gear shock absorption, while nose gear shock absorption is provided by a combination air/oil shock strut.

5. Describe the braking system on this aircraft. (AFM)

Hydraulically actuated disc-type brakes are utilized on each main gear wheel. A hydraulic line connects each brake to a master cylinder located on each pilot's rudder pedals. By applying pressure to the top of either the pilot's or copilot's set of rudder pedals, the brakes may be applied.

6. What type of hydraulic fluid does your aircraft use and what color is it? (FAA-H-8083-25, FAA-H-8083-31)

Refer to your AFM/POH; a mineral-based hydraulic fluid (MIL-H-5606) is the most widely used type for small aircraft. It has an odor similar to penetrating oil and is dyed red. A newer, fire-resistant fluid (MIL-H-83282) is also used in small aircraft and is dyed red.

7. How is steering accomplished on the ground? (AFM)

Light airplanes are generally provided with nosewheel steering capabilities through a simple system of mechanical linkage connected to the rudder pedals. When a rudder pedal is depressed, a spring-loaded bungee (push-pull rod) connected to the pivotal portion of a nosewheel strut will turn the nosewheel.

8. What type of engine does your aircraft have? (AFM)

A horizontally opposed four-cylinder, overhead-valve, air-cooled, carbureted engine. The engine is manufactured by Lycoming and rated at 110 HP.

9. What four strokes must occur in each cylinder of a typical four stroke engine in order for it to produce full power? (FAA-H-8083-25)

The four strokes are:

Intake — begins as the piston starts its downward travel causing the intake valve to open and the fuel-air mixture to be drawn into the cylinder.

Compression — begins when the intake valve closes, and the piston starts moving back to the top of the cylinder. This phase of the cycle is used to obtain a much greater power output from the fuel-air mixture once it is ignited.

Power—begins when the fuel-air mixture is ignited which causes a tremendous pressure increase in the cylinder and forces the piston downward away from the cylinder head, creating the power that turns the crankshaft.

Exhaust—is used to purge the cylinder of burned gases and begins when the exhaust valve opens, and the piston starts to move toward the cylinder head once again.

Remember: Suck, Squeeze, Bang, Blow

10. What does the carburetor do? (FAA-H-8083-25)

Carburetion may be defined as the process of mixing fuel and air in the correct proportions so as to form a combustible mixture. The carburetor vaporizes liquid fuel into small particles and then mixes it with air. It measures the airflow and meters fuel accordingly.

11. How does the carburetor heat system work? (AFM)

A carburetor heat valve, controlled by the pilot, allows unfiltered, heated air from a shroud located around an exhaust riser or muffler to be directed to the induction air manifold prior to the carburetor. Carburetor heat should be used anytime suspected or known carburetor icing conditions exist.

12. What change occurs to the fuel/air mixture when applying carburetor heat? (FAA-H-8083-25)

Normally, the introduction of heated air into the carburetor will result in a richer mixture. Warm air is less dense, resulting in less air for the same amount of fuel. Use of carburetor heat can cause a decrease in engine power of up to 15 percent.

13. What does the throttle do? (FAA-H-8083-25)

The throttle allows the pilot to manually control the amount of fuel/air charge entering the cylinders. This in turn regulates the engine speed and power.

14. What does the mixture control do? (FAA-H-8083-25)

It regulates the fuel-to-air ratio. All airplane engines incorporate a device called a mixture control, by which the fuel/air ratio can be controlled by the pilot during flight. The purpose of a mixture control is to prevent the mixture from becoming too rich at high altitudes, due to decreasing air density. It is also used to lean the mixture during cross-country flights to conserve fuel and provide optimum power.

15. Describe a fuel injection system installed in some aircraft. (FAA-H-8083-25)

The fuel injection system injects fuel directly into the cylinders, or just ahead of the intake valve. It incorporates six basic components:

1. *Engine-driven fuel pump*—provides fuel under pressure from the fuel tank to the fuel/air control unit.

2. *Fuel/air control unit*—meters fuel based on the mixture control setting and sends it to the fuel manifold valve at a rate controlled by the throttle.

3. *Fuel manifold valve*—distributes fuel to the individual fuel discharge nozzles.

4. *Discharge nozzles*—located in each cylinder head, these inject the fuel/air mixture at the precise time for each cylinder directly into each cylinder intake port.

5. *Auxiliary fuel pump*—provides fuel under pressure to fuel/air control unit for engine starting and/or emergency use.

6. *Fuel pressure/flow indicators*—measures metered fuel pressure/flow.

16. What type of ignition system does your airplane have? (AFM)

Engine ignition is provided by two engine-driven magnetos, and two spark plugs per cylinder. The ignition system is completely independent of the aircraft electrical system. The magnetos are engine-driven self-contained units supplying electrical current without using an external source of current. However, before they can produce current, the magnetos must be actuated, as the engine crankshaft is rotated by some other means. To accomplish this, the aircraft battery furnishes electrical power to operate a starter which, through a series of gears, rotates the engine crankshaft. This in turn actuates the armature of the magneto to produce the sparks for ignition of the fuel in each cylinder. After the engine starts, the starter system is disengaged, and the battery no longer contributes to the actual operation of the engine.

17. What are the two main advantages of a dual ignition system? (FAA-H-8083-25)

a. Increased safety: in case one system fails the engine may be operated on the other until a landing is safely made.

b. More complete and even combustion of the mixture, and consequently, improved engine performance; i.e., the fuel/air mixture will be ignited on each side of the combustion chamber and burn toward the center.

18. What type of fuel system does your aircraft have? (AFM)

The fuel system is a "gravity feed" system. Using gravity, the fuel flows from two wing fuel tanks to a fuel shutoff valve which, in the "on" position, allows fuel to flow through a strainer and then to the carburetor. From there, the fuel is mixed with air and then flows into the cylinders through the intake manifold tubes.

19. What purpose do fuel tank vents have? (AFM)

As the fuel level in an aircraft fuel tank decreases, a vacuum would be created within the tank which would eventually result in a decreasing fuel flow and finally engine stoppage. Fuel system venting provides a way of replacing fuel with outside air, preventing formation of a vacuum.

20. Does your aircraft use a fuel pump? (AFM)

No, the fuel is transferred from the wing tanks to the carburetor by the "gravity feed" system. The gravity system does not require a fuel pump because the fuel is always under positive pressure to the carburetor. For some aircraft where for some reason it is not possible to place the wings above the carburetor, or for which a greater pressure is required than what gravity feed can supply, it is necessary to utilize engine-driven fuel pumps and auxiliary fuel pumps as backups.

21. What type fuel does your aircraft require (minimum octane rating and color)? (AFM)

The approved fuel grade used is 100LL and the color is blue.

22. Can other types of fuel be used if the specified grade is not available? (FAA-H-8083-25)

Airplane engines are designed to operate using a specific grade of fuel as recommended by the manufacturer. If the proper grade of fuel is not available, it is possible, but not desirable, to use the next higher grade as a substitute. Always reference the aircraft's AFM or POH. Auto gas should *never* be used in aircraft engines unless the aircraft has been modified with an FAA-issued Supplemental Type Certificate (STC).

23. What color of dye is added to the following fuel grades: 80, 100, 100LL, Turbine? (FAA-H-8083-25, FAA-P-8740-35)

Grade	Color
80 (obsolete)	Red
100 (obsolete)	Green
100LL	Blue
Jet A	Colorless or Straw

24. If a non-turbine piston engine powered airplane is accidentally fueled with JET-A fuel, will it start? (FAA-H-8083-25, FAA-P-8740-35)

Yes. Reciprocating engines may run briefly on jet fuel, but detonation and overheating will soon cause power failure. When an aircraft that requires Avgas is inadvertently fueled with Jet A, there is usually a small amount of Avgas remaining in the aircraft's fuel system (tanks, fuel lines, carburetor, etc.). This remaining fuel can enable an aircraft to taxi, perform an engine run-up, and possibly even take off before experiencing a catastrophic engine failure.

Note: Other than the kerosene smell and the oily feel when rubbed between the fingers, it can be very difficult to visually identify an accidental mixture of 100LL Avgas (blue) and Jet A (straw color).

25. What is the function of the manual primer, and how does it operate? (AFM)

The manual primer's main function is to provide assistance in starting the engine. The primer draws fuel from the fuel strainer and injects it directly into the cylinder intake ports. This usually results in a quicker, more efficient engine start.

26. Describe the electrical system on your aircraft. (AFM)

Electrical energy is provided by a 28-volt, direct-current system powered by an engine-driven 60-amp alternator and a 24-volt battery.

27. How are the circuits for the various electrical accessories within the aircraft protected? (AFM)

Most of the electrical circuits in an airplane are protected from an overload condition by either circuit breakers or fuses or both. Circuit breakers perform the same function as fuses except that when an overload occurs, a circuit breaker can be reset.

28. The electrical system provides power for what equipment in an airplane? (AFM)

Normally, the following:
  a. Radio equipment
  b. Turn coordinator
  c. Fuel gauges
  d. Pitot heat
  e. Landing light
  f. Taxi light
  g. Strobe lights
  h. Interior lights
  i. Instrument lights
  j. Position lights
  k. Flaps (maybe)
  l. Stall warning system (maybe)
  m. Oil temperature gauge
  n. Electric fuel pump (maybe)

29. What does the ammeter indicate? (AFM)

The ammeter indicates the flow of current, in amperes, from the alternator to the battery or from the battery to the electrical system. With the engine running and master switch on, the ammeter will indicate the charging rate to the battery. If the alternator has gone off-line and is no longer functioning, or the electrical load exceeds the output of the alternator, the ammeter indicates the discharge rate of the battery.

30. What function does the voltage regulator have?

The voltage regulator is a device which monitors system voltage, detects changes, and makes the required adjustments in the output of the alternator to maintain a constant regulated system voltage. It must do this at low RPM, such as during taxi, as well as at high RPM in flight. In a 28-volt system, it will maintain 28 volts ±0.5 volts.

31. Why is the generator/alternator voltage output slightly higher than the battery voltage? (FAA-H-8083-25)

The difference in voltage keeps the battery charged. For example, a 12-volt battery would be supplied with 14 volts.

32. How does the aircraft cabin heat work? (AFM)

Fresh air, heated by an exhaust shroud, is directed to the cabin through a series of ducts.

33. How does the pilot control temperature in the cabin? (AFM)

Temperature is controlled by mixing outside air (cabin air control) with heated air (cabin heat control) in a manifold near the cabin firewall. This air is then ducted to vents located on the cabin floor.

34. What are the five basic functions of aircraft engine oil? (FAA-H-8083-25)

Lubricates — the engine's moving parts

Cools — the engine by reducing friction

Removes — heat from the cylinders

Seals—provides a seal between the cylinder walls and pistons

Cleans—by carrying off metal and carbon particles and other oil contaminants

B. System and Equipment Malfunctions

1. What causes "carburetor icing," and what are the first indications of its presence? (FAA-H-8083-25)

The vaporization of fuel, combined with the expansion of air as it passes through the carburetor, causes a sudden cooling of the mixture. The temperature of the air passing through the carburetor may drop as much as 60°F within a fraction of a second. Water vapor is squeezed out by this cooling, and if the temperature in the carburetor reaches 32°F or below, the moisture will be deposited as frost or ice inside the carburetor. For airplanes with a fixed-pitch propeller, the first indication of carburetor icing is loss of RPM. For airplanes with controllable-pitch (constant-speed) propellers, the first indication is usually a drop in manifold pressure.

2. What method is used to determine that carburetor ice has been eliminated? (FAA-H-8083-25)

When heat is first applied, there will be a drop in RPM in airplanes equipped with a fixed-pitch propeller; there will be a drop in manifold pressure in airplanes equipped with a controllable-pitch propeller. If ice is present there will be a rise in RPM or manifold pressure after the initial drop (often accompanied by intermittent engine roughness); and then, when the carburetor heat is turned "off," the RPM or manifold pressure will rise to a setting greater than that before application of heat. The engine should run more smoothly after the ice has been removed.

3. What conditions are favorable for carburetor icing? (FAA-H-8083-25)

Carburetor ice is most likely to occur when temperatures are below 70°F (21°C) and the relative humidity is above 80 percent. However, due to the sudden cooling that takes place in the carburetor, icing can occur even with temperatures as high as 100°F (38°C) and humidity as low as 50 percent. This temperature drop can be as much as 60° to 70°F.

4. Define the terms "anti-icing equipment" and "deicing equipment" and state several examples of each.
(FAA-H-8083-3; FAA-H-8083-25)

Anti-icing equipment—prevents ice from forming on certain protected surfaces. Examples are heated pitot tubes and static ports, carburetor heat, heated fuel vents, propeller blades with electrothermal boots, and heated windshields. It is normally actuated prior to flight into suspected icing conditions. Reference your AFM/POH.

Deicing equipment—removes ice that has already formed on protected surfaces. It is generally limited to pneumatic boots on the wing and tail leading edges.

5. Describe how an aircraft deicing system works.
(FAA-H-8083-3)

Upon pilot actuation, boots attached to the wing leading edges inflate with air from a pneumatic pump(s) to break off accumulated ice. After a few seconds of inflation, they are deflated back to their normal position with vacuum assistance. The pilot monitors the buildup of ice and cycles the boots as directed in the AFM/POH.

6. If an airplane has anti-icing and/or deicing equipment installed, can it be flown into icing conditions?
(FAA-H-8083-3)

Even though it may appear elaborate and complete, the presence of anti-icing and deicing equipment does not necessarily mean that an airplane is approved for flight in icing conditions. The AFM/POH, placards, and even the manufacturer should be consulted for specific determination of approvals and limitations.

7. What is "detonation"? (FAA-H-8083-25)

Detonation is an uncontrolled, explosive ignition of the fuel/air mixture within the cylinder's combustion chamber. It causes excessive temperature and pressure which, if not corrected, can quickly lead to failure of the piston, cylinder, or valves. In less severe cases, detonation causes engine overheating, roughness, or loss of power. Detonation is characterized by high cylinder head temperatures, and is most likely to occur when operating at high power settings.

8. **What are some of the most common operational causes of detonation?** (FAA-8083-25)

   a. Using a lower fuel grade than that specified by the aircraft manufacturer.

   b. Operating with extremely high manifold pressures in conjunction with low RPM.

   c. Operating the engine at high power settings with an excessively lean mixture.

   d. Extended ground operations or steep climbs where cylinder cooling is reduced.

9. **What action should be taken if detonation is suspected?** (FAA-H-8083-25)

   Detonation may be avoided by following these basic guidelines during the various phases of ground and flight operations:

   a. Ensure that the proper grade of fuel is used.

   b. Keep the cowl flaps (if available) in the full-open position while on the ground to provide the maximum airflow through the cowling.

   c. Use an enriched fuel mixture, as well as a shallow climb angle, to increase cylinder cooling during takeoff and initial climb.

   d. Avoid extended, high power, steep climbs.

   e. Develop the habit of monitoring the engine instruments to verify proper operation according to procedures established by the manufacturer.

10. **What is "preignition"?** (FAA-H-8083-25)

    Pre-ignition occurs when the fuel/air mixture ignites prior to the engine's normal ignition event resulting in reduced engine power and high operating temperatures. Premature burning is usually caused by a residual hot spot in the combustion chamber, often created by a small carbon deposit on a spark plug, a cracked spark plug insulator, or other damage in the cylinder that causes a part to heat sufficiently to ignite the fuel/air charge. As with detonation, pre-ignition may also cause severe engine damage, because the expanding gases exert excessive pressure on the piston while still on its compression stroke.

11. What action should be taken if preignition is suspected? (FAA-H-8083-25)

Corrective actions for preignition include any type of engine operation which would promote cooling such as:

a. Reduce power.

b. Reduce the climb rate for better cooling.

c. Enrich the fuel/air mixture.

d. Open cowl flaps if available.

12. During the before-takeoff runup, you switch the magnetos from the "BOTH" position to the "RIGHT" position and notice there is no RPM drop. What condition does this indicate?

The left P-lead is not grounding, or the engine has been running only on the right magneto because the left magneto has totally failed.

13. Interpret the following ammeter indications.

a. Ammeter indicates a right deflection (positive).

- *After starting*—Power from the battery used for starting is being replenished by the alternator; or, if a full-scale charge is indicated for more than 1 minute, the starter is still engaged and a shutdown is indicated.

- *During flight*—A faulty voltage regulator is causing the alternator to overcharge the battery. Reset the system and if the condition continues, terminate the flight as soon as possible.

b. Ammeter indicates a left deflection (negative).

- *After starting*—It is normal during start. At other times this indicates the alternator is not functioning or an overload condition exists in the system. The battery is not receiving a charge.

- *During flight*—The alternator is not functioning or an overload exists in the system. The battery is not receiving a charge. Possible causes: the master switch was accidentally shut off, or the alternator circuit breaker tripped.

14. What action should be taken if the ammeter indicates a continuous discharge while in flight?

The alternator has quit producing a charge, so the alternator circuit breaker should be checked and reset if necessary. If this does not correct the problem, the following should be accomplished:

a. The alternator should be turned off; pull the circuit breaker (the field circuit will continue to draw power from the battery).

b. All electrical equipment not essential to flight should be turned off (the battery is now the only source of electrical power).

c. The flight should be terminated and a landing made as soon as possible.

15. What action should be taken if the ammeter indicates a continuous charge while in flight (more than two needle widths)?

If a continuous excessive rate of charge were allowed for any extended period of time, the battery would overheat and evaporate the electrolyte at an excessive rate. A possible explosion of the battery could result. Also, electronic components in the electrical system would be adversely affected by higher than normal voltage. Protection is provided by an overvoltage sensor which will shut the alternator down if an excessive voltage is detected. If this should occur the following should be done:

a. The alternator should be turned off; pull the circuit breaker (the field circuit will continue to draw power from the battery).

b. All electrical equipment not essential to flight should be turned off (the battery is now the only source of electrical power).

c. The flight should be terminated and a landing made as soon as possible.

16. **During a cross-country flight you notice that the oil pressure is low, but the oil temperature is normal. What is the problem and what action should be taken?**

    A low oil pressure in flight could be the result of any one of several problems, the most common being that of insufficient oil. If the oil temperature continues to remain normal, a clogged oil pressure relief valve or an oil pressure gauge malfunction could be the culprit. In any case, a landing at the nearest airport is advisable to check for the cause of trouble.

17. **What procedures should be followed concerning a partial loss of power in flight?** (AFM)

    If a partial loss of power occurs, the first priority is to establish and maintain a suitable airspeed (best glide airspeed if necessary). Then, select an emergency landing area and remain within gliding distance. As time allows, attempt to determine the cause and correct it.

    Complete the following checklist:

    a. Check the carburetor heat.

    b. Check the amount of fuel in each tank and switch fuel tanks if necessary.

    c. Check the fuel selector valve's current position.

    d. Check the mixture control.

    e. Check that the primer control is all the way in and locked.

    f. Check the operation of the magnetos in all three positions; both, left or right.

18. **What procedures should be followed if an engine fire develops in flight?** (AFM)

    In the event of an engine fire in flight, the following procedures should be used:

    a. Set the mixture control to "Idle cutoff."

    b. Set the fuel selector valve to "Off."

    c. Turn the master switch to "Off."

d. Set the cabin heat and air vents to "Off"; leave the overhead vents "On."

e. Establish an airspeed of 100 KIAS and increase the descent, if necessary, to find an airspeed that will provide for an incombustible mixture.

f. Execute a forced landing procedures checklist.

19. What procedures should be followed if an engine fire develops on the ground during starting? (AFM)

Continue to attempt an engine start as a start will cause flames and excess fuel to be sucked back through the carburetor.

a. If the engine starts:
   • Increase the power to a higher RPM for a few moments; and
   • Shut down the engine and inspect it.

b. If the engine does not start:
   • Set the throttle to the "Full" position.
   • Set the mixture control to "Idle cutoff."
   • Continue to try an engine start in an attempt to put out the fire by vacuum.

c. If the fire continues:
   • Turn the ignition switch to "Off."
   • Turn the master switch to "Off."
   • Set the fuel selector to "Off."

In all cases, evacuate the aircraft and obtain a fire extinguisher and/or assistance.

C. Pitot/Static Flight Instruments

1. What instruments operate off of the pitot/static system? (FAA-H-8083-15)

Altimeter, Vertical Speed, and Airspeed Indicator.

2. How does an altimeter work? (FAA-H-8083-15)

Aneroid wafers expand and contract as atmospheric pressure changes, and through a shaft and gear linkage, rotate pointers on the dial of the instrument.

3. What are the limitations of a pressure altimeter?
(FAA-H-8083-15)

Nonstandard pressure and temperature; temperature variations expand or contract the atmosphere and raise or lower pressure levels that the altimeter senses.

On a warm day—The pressure level is higher than on a standard day. The altimeter indicates lower than actual altitude.

On a cold day—The pressure level is lower than on a standard day. The altimeter indicates higher than actual altitude.

Changes in surface pressure also affect pressure levels at altitude.

Higher than standard pressure—The pressure level is higher than on a standard day. The altimeter indicates lower than actual altitude.

Lower than standard pressure—The pressure level is lower than on a standard day. The altimeter indicates higher than actual altitude.

Remember: High to low or hot to cold, look out below!

4. Define and state how you would determine the following altitudes. (FAA-H-8083-25)

Absolute altitude
Indicated altitude
Pressure altitude
True altitude
Density altitude

Absolute altitude—the vertical distance of an aircraft above the terrain.

Indicated altitude—the altitude read directly from the altimeter (uncorrected) after it is set to the current altimeter setting.

Pressure altitude—the altitude when the altimeter setting window is adjusted to 29.92. Pressure altitude is used for computer solutions to determine density altitude, true altitude, true airspeed, etc.

True altitude—the true vertical distance of the aircraft above sea level. Airport, terrain, and obstacle elevations found on aeronautical charts are true altitudes.

Density altitude—pressure altitude corrected for nonstandard temperature variations. Directly related to an aircraft's takeoff, climb, and landing performance.

5. How does the airspeed indicator operate?
(FAA-H-8083-25)

The airspeed indicator is a sensitive, differential pressure gauge which measures the difference between impact pressure from the pitot head and undisturbed atmospheric pressure from the static source. The difference is registered by the airspeed pointer on the face of the instrument.

6. What is the limitation of the airspeed indicator?
(FAA-H-8083-15)

The airspeed indicator is subject to proper flow of air in the pitot/static system.

7. What are the errors of the airspeed indicator?

Position error—Caused by the static ports sensing erroneous static pressure; slipstream flow causes disturbances at the static port preventing actual atmospheric pressure measurement. It varies with airspeed, altitude and configuration, and may be a plus or minus value.

Density error—Changes in altitude and temperature are not compensated for by the instrument.

Compressibility error—Caused by the packing of air into the pitot tube at high airspeeds, resulting in higher than normal indications. It is usually not a factor at slower speeds.

8. What are the different types of aircraft speeds?
(FAA-H-8083-25)

Indicated Airspeed (IAS)—the speed of the airplane as observed on the airspeed indicator. It is the airspeed without correction for indicator, position (or installation), or compressibility errors.

Calibrated Airspeed (CAS)—the airspeed indicator reading corrected for position (or installation), and instrument errors. CAS is equal to TAS at sea level in standard atmosphere. The color-coding for various design speeds marked on airspeed indicators may be IAS or CAS.

Continued

Equivalent Airspeed (EAS)—the airspeed indicator reading corrected for position (or installation), or instrument error, and for adiabatic compressible flow for the particular altitude. EAS is equal to CAS at sea level in standard atmosphere.

True Airspeed (TAS)—CAS corrected for altitude and nonstandard temperature; the speed of the airplane in relation to the air mass in which it is flying.

9. **Name several important airspeed limitations not marked on the face of the airspeed indicator.** (FAA-H-8083-25)

Design maneuvering speed (V_A)—the maximum speed at which the structural design's limit load can be imposed (either by gusts or full deflection of the control surfaces) without causing structural damage. Note: Operating at or below VA does not provide structural protection against multiple full control inputs in one axis or full control inputs in more than one axis at the same time.

Landing Gear Operating speed (V_{LO})—the maximum speed for extending or retracting the landing gear if using aircraft equipped with retractable landing gear.

Best Angle-of-Climb speed (V_X)—important when a short-field takeoff to clear an obstacle is required.

Best Rate-of-Climb speed (V_Y)—the airspeed that will give the pilot the most altitude in a given period of time.

10. **What airspeed limitations apply to the color-coded marking system of the airspeed indicator?** (FAA-H-8083-25)

White Arc...flap operating range

Lower A/S Limit White Arc ....V_{S0} (stall speed landing configuration)

Upper A/S Limit White Arc ..... V_{FE} (maximum flap extension speed)

Green Arc.. normal operating range

Lower A/S Limit Green Arc .... V_{S1} (stall speed clean or specified configuration)

Upper A/S Limit Green Arc ....V_{NO} (normal operations speed or maximum structural cruise speed)

Yellow Arc .... Caution Range (operations in smooth air only)

Red Line........................ V_{NE} (never exceed speed; above this speed, structural failure may occur.)

11. How does the vertical speed indicator work?
(FAA-H-8083-15)

The vertical speed indicator is a pressure differential instrument. Inside the instrument case is an aneroid very much like the one in an airspeed indicator. Both the inside of this aneroid and the inside of the instrument case are vented to the static system, but the case is vented through a calibrated orifice that causes the pressure inside the case to change more slowly than the pressure inside the aneroid. As the aircraft ascends, the static pressure becomes lower and the pressure inside the case compresses the aneroid, moving the pointer upward, showing a climb and indicating the number of feet per minute the aircraft is ascending.

12. What are the limitations of the vertical speed indicator?
(FAA-H-8083-25)

The VSI is not accurate until the aircraft is stabilized. Because of the restriction in airflow to the static line, a 6 to 9 second lag is required to equalize or stabilize the pressures. Sudden or abrupt changes in aircraft attitude will cause erroneous instrument readings as airflow fluctuates over the static port. Both rough control technique and turbulent air result in unreliable needle indications.

D. Gyroscopic Flight Instruments

1. What instruments contain gyroscopes? (FAA-H-8083-25)

a. the turn coordinator
b. the heading indicator (directional gyro)
c. the attitude indicator (artificial horizon)

2. What are the two fundamental properties of a gyroscope? (FAA-H-8083-25)

Rigidity in space—a gyroscope remains in a fixed position in the plane in which it is spinning.

Precession—the tilting or turning of a gyro in response to a deflective force. The reaction to this force does not occur at the point where it was applied; rather, it occurs at a point that is 90° later in the direction of rotation. The rate at which the gyro precesses is inversely proportional to the speed of the rotor and proportional to the deflective force.

3. What are the various power sources that may be used to power the gyroscopic instruments in an airplane? (FAA-H-8083-25)

In some airplanes, all the gyros are vacuum, pressure, or electrically operated; in others, vacuum or pressure systems provide the power for the heading and attitude indicators, while the electrical system provides the power for the turn coordinator. Most airplanes have at least two sources of power to ensure at least one source of bank information if one power source fails.

4. How does the vacuum system operate? (FAA-H-8083-25)

An engine-driven vacuum pump provides suction which pulls air from the instrument case. Normal pressure entering the case is directed against rotor vanes to turn the rotor (gyro) at high speed, much like a water wheel or turbine operates. Air is drawn into the instrument through a filter from the cockpit and eventually vented outside. Vacuum values vary between manufacturers (usually between 4.5 and 5.5 in. Hg.), but provide rotor speeds from 8,000 to 18,000 RPM.

5. How does the attitude indicator work? (FAA-H-8083-25)

The gyro in the attitude indicator is mounted on a horizontal plane and depends upon rigidity in space for its operation. The horizon bar represents the true horizon. This bar is fixed to the gyro and remains in a horizontal plane as the airplane is pitched or banked about its lateral or longitudinal axis, indicating the attitude of the airplane relative to the true horizon.

6. What are the limitations of an attitude indicator? (FAA-H-8083-25)

The pitch and bank limits depend upon the make and model of the instrument. Limits in the banking plane are usually from 100 degrees to 110 degrees, and the pitch limits are usually from 60 to 70 degrees. If either limit is exceeded, the instrument will tumble or spill and will give incorrect indications until reset. A number of modern attitude indicators will not tumble.

7. What are the errors of the attitude indicator?
(FAA-H-8083-15)

Attitude indicators are free from most errors, but depending upon the speed with which the erection system functions, there may be a slight nose-up indication during a rapid acceleration and a nose-down indication during a rapid deceleration. There is also a possibility of a small bank angle and pitch error after a 180° turn. These inherent errors are small and correct themselves within a minute or so after returning to straight-and-level flight.

8. How does the heading indicator operate?
(FAA-H-8083-25)

The operation of the heading indicator uses the principle of rigidity in space. The rotor turns in a vertical plane, and the compass card is fixed to the rotor. Since the rotor remains rigid in space, the points on the card hold the same position in space relative to the vertical plane. As the instrument case and the airplane revolve around the vertical axis, the card provides clear and accurate heading information.

9. What are the limitations of the heading indicator?
(FAA-H-8083-25)

The bank and pitch limits of the heading indicator vary with the particular design and make of instrument. On some heading indicators found in light airplanes, the limits are approximately 55 degrees of pitch and 55 degrees of bank. When either of these attitude limits is exceeded, the instrument "tumbles" or "spills" and no longer gives the correct indication until reset. After spilling, it may be reset with the caging knob. Many of the modern instruments used are designed in such a manner that they will not tumble.

10. What error is the heading indicator subject to?
(FAA-H-8083-25)

Because of precession, caused chiefly by friction, the heading indicator will creep or drift from a heading to which it is set. Among other factors, the amount of drift depends largely upon the condition of the instrument. The heading indicator may indicate as much as 15° error per every hour of operation.

11. How does the turn coordinator operate? (FAA-H-8083-15)

The turn part of the instrument uses precession to indicate direction and approximate rate of turn. A gyro reacts by trying to move in reaction to the force applied thus moving the needle or miniature aircraft in proportion to the rate of turn. The slip/skid indicator is a liquid-filled tube with a ball that reacts to centrifugal force and gravity.

12. What information does the turn coordinator provide? (FAA-H-8083-25)

The turn coordinator shows the yaw and roll of the aircraft around the vertical and longitudinal axes.

The miniature airplane will indicate direction of the turn as well as rate of turn. When aligned with the turn index, it represents a standard rate of turn of 3° per second. The inclinometer of the turn coordinator indicates the coordination of aileron and rudder. The ball indicates whether the airplane is in coordinated flight or is in a slip or skid.

13. What will the turn indicator indicate when the aircraft is in a "skidding" or a "slipping" turn? (FAA-H-8083-25)

Slip — The ball in the tube will be on the inside of the turn; not enough rate of turn for the amount of bank.

Skid — The ball in the tube will be to the outside of the turn; too much rate of turn for the amount of bank.

E. Magnetic Compass

1. How does the magnetic compass work? (FAA-H-8083-25)

Magnetized needles fastened to a float assembly, around which is mounted a compass card, align themselves parallel to the earth's lines of magnetic force. The float assembly is housed in a bowl filled with acid-free white kerosene.

2. What limitations does the magnetic compass have? (FAA-H-8083-15)

The jewel-and-pivot type mounting allows the float freedom to rotate and tilt up to approximately 18° angle of bank. At steeper bank angles, the compass indications are erratic and unpredictable.

3. What are the various compass errors? (FAA-H-8083-15)

Oscillation error—Erratic movement of the compass card caused by turbulence or rough control technique.

Deviation error—Due to electrical and magnetic disturbances in the aircraft.

Variation error—Angular difference between true and magnetic north; reference isogonic lines of variation.

Dip errors:
Acceleration error—On east or west headings, while accelerating, the magnetic compass shows a turn to the north, and when decelerating, it shows a turn to the south.

Remember: ANDS
   A ccelerate
   N orth
   D ecelerate
   S outh

Northerly turning error—The compass leads in the south half of a turn, and lags in the north half of a turn.

Remember: UNOS
   U ndershoot
   N orth
   O vershoot
   S outh

F. Advanced Avionics

1. Describe the function of the following avionics equipment acronyms: AHRS, ADC, PFD, MFD, FD, FMS, INS. (FAA-H-8083-6, DAT)

AHRS—attitude and heading reference system. Composed of three-axis sensors that provide heading, attitude, and yaw information for aircraft. AHRS are designed to replace traditional mechanical gyroscopic flight instruments and provide superior reliability and accuracy.

ADC—air data computer. An aircraft computer that receives and processes pitot pressure, static pressure, and temperature to calculate precise altitude, indicated airspeed, true airspeed, vertical speed, and air temperature.

PFD—primary flight display. A display that provides increased situational awareness to the pilot by replacing the traditional six instruments with an easy-to-scan display that shows the horizon, airspeed, altitude, vertical speed, trend, trim, rate of turn, and more.

MFD—multi-function display. A cockpit display capable of presenting information (navigation data, moving maps, terrain awareness, etc.) to the pilot in configurable ways; often used in concert with the PFD.

FD—flight director. An electronic flight computer that analyzes the navigation selections, signals, and aircraft parameters. It presents steering instructions on the flight display as command bars or crossbars for the pilot to position the nose of the aircraft over or follow.

FMS—flight management system. A computer system containing a database for programming of routes, approaches, and departures that can supply navigation data to the flight director/autopilot from various sources, and can calculate flight data such as fuel consumption, time remaining, possible range, and other values.

INS—inertial navigation system. A computer-based navigation system that tracks the movement of an aircraft via signals produced by onboard accelerometers. The initial location of the aircraft is entered into the computer and all subsequent movement is then sensed and used to keep the aircraft's position updated.

2. What is the function of a magnetometer? (FAA-H-8083-6)

A magnetometer is a device that measures the strength of the earth's magnetic field to determine aircraft heading; it provides this information digitally to the AHRS, which then sends it to the PFD.

3. When powering up an aircraft with an FMS/RNAV unit installed, how will you verify the effective dates of the navigation database? (FAA-H-8083-6)

The effective dates for the navigation database are typically shown on a start-up screen that is displayed as the system cycles through its startup self-test.

4. Does an aircraft have to remain stationary during AHRS system initialization? (FAA-H-8083-6)

Some AHRSs must be initialized on the ground prior to departure. The initialization procedure allows the system to establish a reference attitude used as a benchmark for all future attitude changes. Other systems are capable of initialization while taxiing as well as in flight.

5. Which standby flight instruments are normally provided in an advanced avionics aircraft? (FAA-H-8083-6)

Every aircraft equipped with electronic flight instruments must also contain a minimal set of backup/standby instruments. Usually conventional "round dial instruments," they typically include an attitude indicator, an airspeed indicator, and an altimeter.

6. If one display fails (PFD or MFD), what information will be presented on the remaining display? (FAA-H-8083-6)

In the event of a display failure, some systems offer a reversion capability to display the primary flight instruments and engine instruments on the remaining operative display.

7. When a display failure occurs, what other system components will be affected? (AFM/POH)

In some systems, failure of a display will also result in partial loss of navigation, communication, and GPS capability. Reference your specific AFM/POH.

8. **What display information will be affected when an ADC failure occurs?** (FAA-H-8083-6)

   Inoperative airspeed, altitude, and vertical speed indicators, shown with red Xs on the PFD, indicate the failure of the air data computer.

9. **What display information will be lost when an AHRS failure occurs?** (FAA-H-8083-6)

   An inoperative attitude indicator, shown with a red X on the PFD, indicates failure of the AHRS.

10. **How will loss of a magnetometer affect the AHRS operation?** (FAA-H-8083-6)

    Heading information will be lost.

    Exam Tip: Be prepared to answer questions about any and all equipment installed in the aircraft. For example, if your aircraft has an autopilot, have in-depth knowledge of its operation, even if you rarely use it.

Additional Study Questions

1. Does the nose wheel turn when the rudder is depressed in flight? (AFM)

2. If the braking system is not functioning, will the parking brake work? (AFM)

3. If the brakes on the left side (pilot) are not functioning, will the brakes on the right side also be inoperative? (AFM)

4. Explain the procedure for starting your airplane with external power. (AFM)

5. You cannot start your airplane due to a low battery, so you request an external start via a ground power cart. What problems might still occur after the engine has started? (AFM)

6. In the event of an electrical system failure, what time duration can you reasonably expect electrical power from the battery? (AFM)

7. What effect would positioning the master switch to the "Off" position have on aircraft systems while in flight? (FAA-H-8083-25)

8. What instruments are affected when the pitot tube freezes? Static port freezes? (FAA-H-8083-25)

9. What is the purpose of the alternate static source? (FAA-H-8083-25)

10. If you set the altimeter from 29.15 to 29.85, what change occurs? (FAA-H-8083-25)

11. During the "before takeoff" magneto check, you notice that the right magneto is extremely rough. Explain what the problem could be and what actions you will take next. (AFM)

12. **Automation in the cockpit has made aviation safer. Does total risk increase or decrease when "passively" monitoring an automated system for faults or abnormalities? How can you mitigate that risk?** (FAA-H-8083-2)

Cross-Country
Flight Planning

6

A. Navigation

1. What are three common ways to navigate?

To navigate successfully, pilots must know their approximate position at all times or be able to determine it whenever they wish. Position may be determined by:

a. Pilotage (by reference to visible landmarks);

b. Dead reckoning (by computing direction and distance from a known position); or

c. Radio navigation (by use of radio aids).

2. What type of aeronautical charts are available for use in VFR navigation? (AIM 9-1-4)

a. *Sectional Charts*—designed for visual navigation of slow to medium speed aircraft. One inch equals 6.86 nautical miles. They are revised semiannually, except most Alaskan charts which are revised annually.

b. *VFR Terminal Area Charts (TAC)*—TACs depict the Class B airspace. While similar to sectional charts, TACs have more detail because the scale is larger. One inch equals 3.43 nautical miles. Charts are revised semiannually, except in Puerto Rico and the Virgin Islands where they are revised annually.

c. *VFR Flyway Planning Charts*—This chart is printed on the reverse side of selected TAC charts. The coverage is the same as the associated TAC. They depict flight paths and altitudes recommended for use to bypass high traffic areas.

3. Are electronic flight bags (EFBs) approved for use as a replacement for paper reference material (POH and Supplements, charts, etc.) in the cockpit? (AC 91-78)

Yes. EFBs can be used during all phases of flight operations in lieu of paper reference material when the information displayed is the functional equivalent of the paper reference material replaced and is current, up-to-date, and valid. It is recommended that a secondary or back-up source of aeronautical information necessary for the flight be available.

4. Be capable of locating the following items on a sectional chart:

Abandoned airports

Air Defense Identification Zone (ADIZ)

Airport elevation

Airports with a rotating beacon

Airports with lighting facilities

Airports with services

Alert Area

Approach Control frequencies

ATIS

Class B airspace

Class C airspace

Class D airspace

Class D airspace ceiling

Class E airspace (controlled airspace 700 foot floor)

Class E airspace (controlled airspace 1,200 foot floor)

Class E surface area

Class E transition area

Class G airspace

CTAF

Flight Service Station frequencies

Glider operating area

Hard surfaced runway airports

HIWAS

IFR route

Isogonic lines

Maximum elevation figures

Military Airports

Military Operations Area

Military Training Routes

Mode C veil

National Security Area

No fixed-wing Special VFR available

Non-hard surfaced runways

Non-directional radio beacons
Non-tower controlled airport
Obstructions above 1,000 feet AGL
Obstructions below 1,000 feet AGL
Parachute Jumping Area
Part-time lighting
Pilot Controlled Lighting
Private airports
Prohibited area
Restricted area
Runway length
Special Conservation Area
Special Flight Rules Area
UNICOM frequencies
VFR transition route
VFR waypoint
Victor airways
Visual check points
VORTAC
Warning area
TRSA (Terminal Radar Service Area) if available

5. What is an "isogonic line"? (FAA-H-8083-25)

Shown on most aeronautical charts as broken magenta lines, iso-gonic lines connect points of equal magnetic variation. They show the amount and direction of magnetic variation, which from time to time may vary.

6. What is "magnetic variation"? (FAA-H-8083-25)

Variation is the angle between true north and magnetic north. It is expressed as east variation or west variation depending upon whether magnetic north (MN) is to the east or west of true north (TN), respectively.

7. How do you convert a true direction to a magnetic direction? (FAA-H-8083-25)

To convert true course or heading to magnetic course or heading, note the variation shown by the nearest isogonic line. If variation is west, add; if east, subtract.

Remember: East is Least (Subtract)
        West is Best (Add)

8. What are lines of latitude and longitude? (FAA-H-8083-25)

Circles parallel to the equator (lines running east and west), parallels of latitude, enable us to measure distance in degrees latitude north or south of the equator. Meridians of longitude are drawn from the North Pole to the South Pole and are at right angles to the equator. The "Prime Meridian," which passes through Greenwich, England, is used as the zero line from which measurements are made in degrees east and west to 180°. The 48 conterminous states of the United States lie between 25 degrees and 49 degrees north latitude and between 67 degrees and 125 degrees west longitude.

9. What is "magnetic deviation"? (FAA-H-8083-25)

Because of magnetic influences within the airplane itself (electrical circuits, radios, lights, tools, engine, magnetized metal parts, etc.) the compass needle is frequently deflected from its normal reading. This deflection is called deviation. Deviation is different for each airplane, and also varies for different headings of the same airplane. The deviation value may be found on a deviation card located in the airplane.

10. Name several types of navigational aids. (AIM 1-1-2 through 1-1-7 and 1-1-17)

a. VOR (Very High Frequency Omnidirectional Range)

b. VORTAC (VHF Omnidirectional Range/Tactical Air Navigation)

c. DME (Distance Measuring Equipment)

d. RNAV (Area Navigation) includes INS, VOR/DME-referenced, and GPS.

11. What is a "VOR" or "VORTAC"? (FAA-H-8083-25)

VORs are VHF radio stations that project radials in all directions (360°) from the station, like spokes from the hub of a wheel. Each of these radials is denoted by its outbound magnetic direction. Almost all VOR stations will also be VORTACs. A VORTAC (VOR-Tactical Air Navigation), provides the standard bearing information of a VOR plus distance information to pilots of airplanes which have distance measuring equipment (DME).

12. Within what frequency range do VORs operate? (FAA-H-8083-25)

Transmitting frequencies of omnirange stations are in the VHF (very high frequency) band between 108 and 117.95 MHz, which are immediately below aviation communication frequencies.

13. What is a VOR "radial"? (FAA-H-8083-25)

A "radial" is defined as a line of magnetic bearing extending from an omnidirectional range (VOR). A VOR projects 360 radials from the station. These radials are always identified by their direction "from" the station. Regardless of heading, an aircraft on the 360° radial will always be located north of the station.

14. How are VOR NAVAIDs classified? (AIM 1-1-8)

Terminal, Low, and High

15. What reception distances can be expected from the various class VORs? (FAA-H-8083-25)

Class	Distance/Altitudes	Miles
T	12,000' and below	25
L	Below 18,000'	40
H	Below 18,000'	40
H	14,500 – 17,999'	100 (conterminous 48 states only)
H	18,000 – FL450	130
H	Above FL450	100

16. What limitations, if any, apply to VOR reception distances? (AIM 1-1-3)

VORs are subject to line-of-sight restrictions, and the range varies proportionally to the altitude of the receiving equipment.

17. **What are the different methods for checking the accuracy of VOR receiver equipment?** (14 CFR 91.171)

    a. VOT check—plus or minus 4°

    b. Ground checkpoint—plus or minus 4°

    c. Airborne checkpoint—plus or minus 6°

    d. Dual VOR check—4° between each other

    e. Selected radial over a known ground point—plus or minus 6°

18. **What is "DME"?** (AIM 1-1-7)

    Distance Measuring Equipment (airborne and ground)—used to measure, in nautical miles, the slant range distance of an aircraft from the DME navigational aid. Aircraft equipped with DME are provided with distance and ground speed information when receiving a VORTAC or TACAN facility. DME operates on frequencies in the UHF spectrum between 960 MHz and 1215 MHz.

19. **Give a brief explanation of GPS.** (AIM 1-1-17)

    Global positioning system (GPS) is a satellite-based radio navigation system that broadcasts a signal used by receivers to determine a precise position anywhere in the world. The receiver tracks multiple satellites and determines a pseudo-range measurement that is then used to determine the user's location.

20. **What are the three functional elements of GPS?** (FAA-H-8083-15)

    Space element—consists of 30 satellites.

    Control element—consists of a network of ground-based GPS monitoring and control stations that ensure the accuracy of satellite positions and their clocks.

    User element—consists of antennas and receiver-processors onboard aircraft that provide positioning, velocity, and precise timing to the user.

21 What are the different types of GPS receivers available for use? (AIM 1-1-17)

GPS receivers used for VFR navigation vary from fully integrated IFR/VFR installations used to support VFR operations, to hand-held devices. Pilots must understand the limitations of the receivers prior to using in flight to avoid misusing navigation information.

22. What is the purpose of RAIM? (FAA-H-8083-6)

Receiver autonomous integrity monitoring (RAIM) is a self-monitoring function performed by a GPS receiver to ensure that adequate GPS signals are being received from the satellites at all times. The GPS will alert the pilot whenever the integrity monitoring determines that the GPS signals do not meet the criteria for safe navigational use.

23. Where can a pilot obtain RAIM availability information? (AIM 1-1-17)

Pilots may obtain GPS RAIM availability information by using a manufacturer-supplied RAIM prediction tool, or using the Service Availability Prediction Tool (SAPT) on the FAA enroute and terminal RAIM prediction website. Pilots can also request GPS RAIM aeronautical information from an FSS during preflight briefings.

24. If RAIM capability is lost in-flight, can you continue to use GPS for navigation? (FAA-H-8083-25, AIM 1-1-17)

Without RAIM capability, the pilot has no assurance of the accuracy of the GPS position. VFR GPS panel-mount receivers and handheld units have no RAIM alerting capability. This prevents the pilot from being alerted to the loss of the required number of satellites in view, or the detection of a position error.

25. Before conducting a flight using GPS equipment for navigation, what basic preflight checks should be made? (FAA-H-8083-16)

a. Verify that the GPS equipment is properly installed and certified for the planned operation.

b. Verify that the databases (navigation, terrain, obstacle, etc.) have not expired.

Continued

   c. Review GPS NOTAM/RAIM information related to the planned route of flight.

   d. Review operational status of ground-based NAVAIDs and related aircraft equipment (e.g., 30-day VOR check) appropriate to route of flight.

   e. Determine that the GPS receiver operation manual or airplane flight manual supplement is onboard and available for use.

26. How can a pilot determine what type of operation a GPS receiver is approved for? (FAA-H-8083-6)

The pilot should reference the POH/AFM and supplements to determine the limitations and operating procedures for the particular GPS equipment installed. Most systems require that the avionics operations manual/handbook be on board as a limitation of use.

27. During a preflight briefing, will the FSS briefer automatically provide a pilot with GPS NOTAMS? (FAA-H-8083-6)

No. You must specifically request GPS/WAAS NOTAMs.

28. How many satellites does a GPS receiver require to compute its position? (FAA-H-8083-15)

3 satellites—yields a latitude and longitude position only (2D)

4 satellites—yields latitude, longitude, and altitude position (3D)

5 satellites—3D and RAIM

6 satellites—3D and RAIM (isolates corrupt signal and removes from navigation solution)

29. What is WAAS? (FAA-H-8083-6)

The wide area augmentation system (WAAS) is a ground and satellite integrated navigational error correction system that provides accuracy enhancements to signals received from the global positioning system. WAAS provides extremely accurate lateral and vertical navigation signals to aircraft equipped with GPS/WAAS-enabled certified (TSO C-146) equipment.

30. What limitations should you be aware of when using a panel-mount VFR GPS or a hand-held VFR GPS system for navigation? (AIM 1-1-17)

a. *RAIM capability*—Many VFR GPS receivers and all hand-held units have no RAIM alerting capability. Loss of the required number of satellites in view, or the detection of a position error, cannot be displayed to the pilot by such receivers.

b. *Database currency*—In many receivers, an updatable database is used for navigation fixes, airports, and instrument procedures. These databases must be maintained to the current update for IFR operation, but no such requirement exists for VFR use.

c. *Antenna location*—In many VFR installations of GPS receivers, antenna location is more a matter of convenience than performance. Handheld GPS receiver antenna location is limited to the cockpit or cabin only and is rarely optimized to provide a clear view of available satellites. Loss of signal, coupled with a lack of RAIM capability, could present erroneous position and navigation information with no warning to the pilot.

31. Define the term "VFR waypoint." (FAA-H-8083-25)

VFR waypoints provide pilots with a supplementary tool to assist with position awareness while navigating visually in aircraft equipped with area navigation receivers (such as GPS). They provide navigational aids for pilots unfamiliar with an area, waypoint definition of existing reporting points, enhanced navigation in and around Class B and Class C airspace, and around special use airspace. VFR waypoint names consist of a five-letter identifier beginning with "VP" and are retrievable from navigation databases; they should be used only when operating under VFR conditions.

B. Flight Computers and Basic Calculations

1. Before attempting a cross-country flight, a pilot will need to know how to make common calculations for time, speed, distance, amount of fuel required, as well as basic wind calculations. Solve the following:

Time, speed and distance problems:

a. If time equals 25 minutes and distance equals 47 NM, what will speed be?

b. If distance equals 84 NM and speed equals 139 knots, what will time be?

c. If speed is 85 knots and time is 51 minutes, what will the distance be?

    a. 113 knots

    b. 36 minutes

    c. 72 NM

Fuel consumption problems:

a. If gallons-per-hour is 9.3 and time is 1 hour, 27 minutes, how many gallons will be consumed?

b. If time is 2 hours, 13 minutes and gallons consumed is 32, what will the gallons-per-hour be?

c. If gallons consumed is 38 and gallons-per-hour is 10.8, what will the time be?

    a. 13.5 gallons

    b. 14.4 GPH

    c. 3 hours, 31 minutes

True airspeed problems:

  a. If altitude is 10,000 feet, temperature is 0°C, and IAS is 115, what will the TAS be?

  b. If IAS is 103, altitude is 6,000 feet, and the temperature is -10°C, what will the TAS be?

  c. If the temperature is 40°F, the IAS is 115, and the altitude is 11,000 feet, what will the TAS be?

  a. 135 TAS

  b. 110 TAS

  c. 139 TAS

Density altitude problems:

  a. If pressure altitude is 1,500 feet and the temperature is 35°C, what will the density altitude be?

  b. If pressure altitude is 5,000 feet and the temperature is -10°C, what will the density altitude be?

  c. If the pressure altitude is 2,000 feet and the temperature is 30°C, what will the density altitude be?

  a. 4,100 feet

  b. 3,100 feet

  c. 4,200 feet

Conversion problems:

  a. 100 nautical miles = _____ statute miles

  b. 12 quarts oil = _____ pounds

  c. 45 gallons fuel = _____ pounds

  d. 80°F = _____ °C

  e. 20 knots = _____ miles per hour

  a. 115 SM

  b. 22.5 pounds

  c. 270 pounds

  d. 26.6°C

  e. 23 MPH

Ground speed/true heading problems:

a. **If wind direction is 220, wind speed is 030, true course is 146, and TAS is 135, what will ground speed and true heading be?**

b. **If wind direction is 240, wind speed is 025, true course is 283 and TAS is 165, what will ground speed and true heading be?**

c. **If wind direction is 060, wind speed is 030, true course is 036 and TAS is 140, what will ground speed and true heading be?**

   a. Ground speed is 124, true heading is 158.

   b. Ground speed is 146, true heading is 277.

   c. Ground speed is 112, true heading is 041.

2. **Flight log example, VFR flight plan:**

   Careful preflight planning is extremely important. A wise pilot ensures a successful cross-country flight by getting a good preflight briefing, completing a flight log, and filing a flight plan before flight.

   a. Get a preflight briefing consisting of the latest or most current weather, airport, and enroute NAVAID information.

   b. Draw course lines and mark checkpoints on the chart.

   c. Enter checkpoints on the log.

   d. Enter NAVAIDs on the log.

   e. Enter VOR courses on the log.

   f. Enter altitude on the log.

   g. Enter the wind (direction/velocity) and temperature on the log.

   h. Measure the true course on the chart and enter it on the log.

   i. Compute the true airspeed and enter it on the log.

   j. Compute the WCA and GS and enter them on the log.

   k. Determine variation from chart and enter it on the log.

   l. Determine deviation from compass correction card and enter it on the log.

   m. Enter compass heading on the log.

n. Measure distances on the chart and enter them on the log.

o. Figure ETE and ETA and enter them on the log.

p. Calculate fuel burn and usage; enter them on the log.

q. Compute weight and balance.

r. Compute takeoff and landing performance.

s. Complete a Flight Plan form.

t. File the Flight Plan with FSS.

3. After takeoff, you attempt to activate you VFR flight plan but are unable to contact the FSS. What will happen to your filed flight plan? (FAA-H-8083-25)

When a VFR flight plan is filed, it is held by the FSS until 1 hour after the proposed departure time and then is canceled.

4. Diversion to Alternate/Lost Procedures:

a. What actions should be taken if you become disoriented or lost on a cross-country flight (no GPS available)?

Condition I: plenty of fuel and weather conditions good.

- Straighten up and fly right. Fly a specific heading in a direction you believe to be correct (or circle, if unsure); don't wander aimlessly.

- If you have been flying a steady compass heading and keeping a relatively accurate navigation log, it's not likely you will have a problem locating your position.

- If several VORs are within reception distance, use them for a cross-bearing to determine position (even a single VOR can be of enormous help in narrowing down your possible position); or, fly to the station—there's no doubt where you are then.

- Use knowledge of your last known position, elapsed time, approximate wind direction and ground speed, to establish how far you may have traveled since your last checkpoint.

- Use this distance as a radius and draw a semicircle ahead of your last known position on chart. For example, you estimate your ground speed at 120 knots. If you have been flying 20

Continued

minutes since your last checkpoint, then the no-wind radius of your semicircle is 40 miles projected along the direction of your estimated track.

- If still unsure of your position, loosen up the eyeballs and start some first-class pilotage. Look for something big. Don't concern yourself with the minute or trivial at this point. Often, there will be linear features such as rivers, mountain ranges, or prominent highways and railroads that are easy to identify. You can use them simply as references for orientation purposes and thus find them of great value in fixing your approximate position.

Condition II: low on fuel; weather deteriorating; inadequate experience; darkness imminent; and/or equipment malfunctioning.

Get it on the ground! Most accidents are the product of mistakes which have multiplied over a period of time and getting lost is no exception: don't push your luck. It may well be that in doing so, you have added the final mistake which will add another figure to the accident statistics. If terrain or other conditions make landing impossible at the moment, don't waste time, for it is of the essence: don't search for the perfect field—anything usable will do. Remember, most people on the ground know where they are, and you know that you do not.

b. If it becomes apparent that you cannot locate your position, what action is recommended at this point?

The FAA recommends the use of the "4 Cs":

- *Climb*—The higher altitude allows better communication capability as well as better visual range for identification of landmarks.
- *Communicate*—Use the system. Use 121.5 MHz if no other frequency produces results. It is guarded by FSS's, control towers, military towers, approach control facilities, and Air Route Traffic Control Centers.
- *Confess*—Once communications are established, let them know your problem.
- *Comply*—Follow instructions.

c. While en route on a cross-country flight, weather has deteriorated and it has become necessary to divert to an alternate airport. Assuming no GPS or DME capability, describe how you will navigate to the alternate.
(FAA-H-8083-25)

- After selecting my alternate, I will approximate the magnetic course to the alternate using a straight edge and a compass rose from a nearby VOR or an airway that closely parallels my direction to the alternate.
- I can use the straight edge and scale at the bottom of the chart to approximate a distance to the alternate. I can fine-tune this course and distance later, as time permits, with a plotter.
- If time permits, I'll start my diversion over a prominent ground feature. However, in an emergency, I will divert promptly toward my alternate.

Note: Attempting to complete all plotting, measuring, and computations involved before diverting to the alternate destination may only aggravate an actual emergency.

- Once established on course, I'll note the time, and then use the winds aloft nearest to my diversion point to calculate a heading and GS. Once I have my GS, I'll determine my ETA and fuel consumption to the alternate.
- I'll give priority to flying the aircraft while dividing attention between navigation and planning.
- When determining my altitude to use while diverting, I'll consider cloud heights, winds, terrain, and radio reception.

C. Radio Communications

1. What is the most common type of communication radio equipment installed in general aviation aircraft? How many channels are available? (FAA-H-8083-25)

In general aviation, the most common types of radios are VHF. A VHF radio operates on frequencies between 118.0 and 136.975 MHz and is classified as 720 or 760 depending on the number of channels it can accommodate. The 720 and 760 uses .025 spacing (118.025, 118.050, etc.) with the 720 having a frequency range up to 135.975 and the 760 going up to 136.975.

2. What is the universal VHF "Emergency" frequency? (AIM 5-6-13 and 6-3-1)

121.5 MHz; this frequency is guarded by military towers, most civil towers, FSS's, and radar facilities.

Note: All aircraft operating in the U.S. national airspace are highly encouraged to maintain a listening watch on VHF/UHF guard frequencies (121.5 or 243.0 MHz).

3. What frequencies are used for ground control? (AIM 4-3-14)

The majority of ground control frequencies are 121.6 to 121.9 MHz.

4. What is a "CTAF"? (AIM 4-1-9)

A CTAF (Common Traffic Advisory Frequency) is a frequency designated for the purpose of carrying out airport advisory practices while operating to or from an airport without an operating control tower. The CTAF may be a UNICOM, MULTICOM, FSS or TOWER frequency and is identified in appropriate aeronautical publications.

5. What is "UNICOM," and what frequencies are designated for its use? (AIM 4-1-9 and 4-1-11)

UNICOM is a nongovernment communication facility which may provide airport information at certain airports. Airports other than those with a control tower/FSS on airport will normally use 122.700, 122.725, 122.800, 122.975, 123.000, 123.050, and 123.075 MHz. Airports with a control tower or an FSS on airport will normally use 122.950 MHz.

6. What does "ATIS" mean? (AIM 4-1-13)

Automatic Terminal Information Service (ATIS) is the continuous broadcast of recorded noncontrol information in selected high-activity terminal areas. Its purpose is to improve controller effectiveness and to relieve frequency congestion by automating the repetitive transmission of essential but routine information.

7. If operating into an airport without an operating control tower, FSS or UNICOM, what procedure should be followed? (AIM 4-1-9, Glossary)

Where there is no tower, FSS, or UNICOM station on the airport, use MULTICOM frequency 122.9 for self-announce procedures. MULTICOM is a mobile service not open to public use, used to provide communications essential to conduct the activities being performed by or directed from private aircraft.

8. What frequencies are monitored by most FSS's other than 121.5? (AIM 4-2-14)

FSS's and supplemental weather service locations (SWSL) have assigned frequencies for their different functions. For example, in Alaska, certain FSS's provide local airport advisory on 123.6 MHz, or other frequencies that can be found in the *Chart Supplement U.S.* If in doubt about what to use, 122.2 MHz is designated as a common enroute simplex frequency at most FSS's.

Exam Tip: Be prepared to explain how you will obtain updated weather information while en route. Know how to contact an FSS along your route of flight.

9. What is an RCO? (AIM Glossary)

A remote communications outlet (RCO) is an unmanned communications facility remotely controlled by ATC personnel, established for the purpose of providing ground-to-ground communications between ATC and pilots located at satellite airports. ATC may use the RCO to deliver en route clearances and departure authorizations, and to acknowledge IFR cancellations or departure/landing times. As a secondary function, RCOs may be used for advisory purposes whenever the aircraft is below the coverage of the primary air/ground frequency.

10. How can a pilot determine what frequency is appropriate for activating his/her VFR flight plan once airborne?

Two ways:

a. Ask the FSS briefer during the preflight weather briefing.

b. Consult the communications section under flight service for the airport of departure in the *Chart Supplement U.S.*

11. What is the meaning of a heavy-lined blue box surrounding a NAVAID frequency? (Chart Legend)

A heavy-lined blue box surrounding the NAVAID station data indicates FSS frequencies 121.5, 122.2, 243.0 and 255.4 are available.

12. Why would a frequency be printed on top of a heavy-lined box? (Chart Legend)

This usually means that this frequency is available in addition to the standard FSS frequencies.

13. What is the meaning of a thin-lined blue box surrounding a NAVAID frequency? (Chart Legend)

A plain box without frequencies on top indicates that there are no standard FSS frequencies available. These NAVAIDs will have a "no voice" symbol (underline under frequency).

14. Why would a frequency be printed on top of a thin-lined blue box? (Chart Legend)

These frequencies are the best frequencies to use in the immediate vicinity of the NAVAID site, and will ensure reception by the controlling FSS at low altitudes without terrain interference. They will normally be followed by an "R" which indicates that the FSS can receive only on that frequency (you transmit on that frequency). The pilot will listen for a response over the NAVAID frequency.

15. How can a pilot determine the availability of HIWAS when looking at a VFR Sectional chart? (FAA-H-8083-25)

Navaids that have HIWAS capability are depicted on sectional charts with an "H" in the upper right corner of the identification box.

16. What meaning does the letter "T" in a solid blue circle appearing in the top right corner of a NAVAID frequency box have? (Chart Legend)

(Alaska only) A Transcribed Weather Broadcast is available. A TWEB is a continuous recording of meteorological and aeronautical information that is broadcast on L/MF and VOR facilities for pilots.

D. Federal Aviation Regulations Part 91

1. If an inflight emergency requires immediate action by the pilot, what authority and responsibilities does he/she have? (14 CFR 91.3)

a. The PIC is directly responsible for, and is the final authority as to, the operation of that aircraft.

b. In an inflight emergency requiring immediate action, the PIC may deviate from any rule in Part 91 to the extent required to meet that emergency.

c. Each PIC who deviates from a Part 91 rule shall, upon request from the Administrator, send a written report of that deviation to the Administrator.

2. What restrictions apply to pilots concerning the use of drugs and alcohol? (14 CFR 91.17)

No person may act or attempt to act as a crewmember of a civil aircraft:

a. within 8 hours after the consumption of any alcoholic beverage;

b. while under the influence of alcohol;

c. while using any drug that affects the person's faculties in any way contrary to safety; or

d. while having an alcohol concentration of .04 percent or more in a blood or breath specimen.

3. Is it permissible for a pilot to allow a person who is obviously under the influence of intoxicating liquors or drugs to be carried aboard an aircraft? (14 CFR 91.17)

No. Except in an emergency, no pilot of a civil aircraft may allow a person who appears to be intoxicated or who demonstrates by manner or physical indications that the individual is under the influence of drugs (except a medical patient under proper care) to be carried in that aircraft.

4. **May portable electronic devices be operated onboard an aircraft?** (14 CFR 91.21)

   Aircraft operated by a holder of an air carrier operating certificate or an aircraft operating under IFR may not allow operation of electronic devices onboard their aircraft. Exceptions are: portable voice recorders, hearing aids, heart pacemakers, electric shavers, or any other device that the operator of the aircraft has determined will not cause interference with the navigation or communication system of the aircraft on which it is to be used.

5. **Under what conditions may objects be dropped from an aircraft?** (14 CFR 91.15)

   No pilot-in-command of a civil aircraft may allow any object to be dropped from that aircraft in flight that creates a hazard to persons or property. However, this section does not prohibit the dropping of any object if reasonable precautions are taken to avoid injury or damage to persons or property.

6. **Concerning a flight in the local area, is any preflight action required, and if so, what must it consist of?** (14 CFR 91.103)

   Yes, pilots must familiarize themselves with all available information concerning that flight, including runway lengths at airports of intended use, and takeoff and landing distance data under existing conditions.

7. **Preflight action as required by regulation for all flights away from the vicinity of the departure airport shall include a review of what specific information?** (14 CFR 91.103)

   For a flight under IFR or a flight not in the vicinity of an airport—
   N OTAMs
   W eather reports and forecasts
   K nown ATC traffic delays
   R unway lengths at airports of intended use
   A lternatives available if the planned flight cannot be completed
   F uel requirements
   T akeoff and landing distance data

8. Which persons on board an aircraft are required to use seatbelts and when? (14 CFR 91.107)

Each person on board a U.S.-registered civil aircraft must occupy an approved seat or berth with a safety belt, and if installed, shoulder harness, properly secured about him or her during movement on the surface, takeoff and landing. However a person who has not reached his or her second birthday and does not occupy or use any restraining device may be held by an adult who is occupying a seat or berth, and a person on board for the purpose of engaging in sport parachuting may use the floor of the aircraft as a seat.

9. What responsibility does the pilot-in-command have concerning passengers and their use of seatbelts? (14 CFR 91.107)

No pilot may take off a U.S. registered civil aircraft unless the pilot-in-command of that aircraft ensures that each person on board is briefed on how to fasten and unfasten that person's safety belt and shoulder harness, if installed. The pilot-in-command shall ensure that all persons on board have been notified to fasten their seatbelt and shoulder harness, if installed, before movement of the aircraft on the surface, takeoff or landing.

10. When are flight crewmembers required to keep their seatbelts and shoulder harnesses fastened? (14 CFR 91.105)

During takeoff and landing, and while en route, each required flight crewmember shall keep his/her seatbelt fastened while at his/her station. During takeoff and landing this includes shoulder harnesses, if installed, unless it interferes with other required duties.

11. If operating an aircraft in close proximity to another, such as formation flight, what regulations apply? (14 CFR 91.111)

a. No person may operate an aircraft so close to another aircraft as to create a collision hazard.

b. No person may operate an aircraft in formation flight except by arrangement with the pilot-in-command of each aircraft in the formation.

c. No person may operate an aircraft, carrying passengers for hire, in formation flight.

12. What is the order of right-of-way as applied to the different categories of aircraft? (14 CFR 91.113)

B alloons
G liders
A irships
A irplanes
R otorcraft

Aircraft towing or refueling other aircraft have the right-of-way over all other engine-driven aircraft.

Remember: BGAAR (BIG "R")

13. When would an aircraft have the right-of-way over all other air traffic? (14 CFR 91.113)

An aircraft in distress has the right-of-way over all other air traffic.

14. State the required action for each of the aircraft confrontations (same category), below. (14 CFR 91.113)

Converging

Approaching head-on

Overtaking

Converging—aircraft on right has the right-of-way.

Approaching head-on—both aircraft shall alter course to right.

Overtaking—aircraft being overtaken has the right-of-way; pilot of the overtaking aircraft shall alter course to the right.

15. What right-of-way rules apply when two or more aircraft are approaching an airport for the purpose of landing? (14 CFR 91.113)

Aircraft on final approach to land or while landing have the right-of-way over aircraft in flight or operating on the surface, except that they shall not take advantage of this rule to force an aircraft off the runway surface which has already landed and is attempting to make way for an aircraft on final approach. When two or more aircraft are approaching an airport for the purpose of landing, the aircraft at the lower altitude has the right-of-way, but it shall not take advantage of this rule to cut in front of another which is on final approach to land or to overtake that aircraft.

16. **Unless otherwise authorized or required by ATC, what is the maximum indicated airspeed at which a person may operate an aircraft below 10,000 feet MSL?** (14 CFR 91.117)

    No person may operate an aircraft below 10,000 feet MSL at an indicated airspeed of more than 250 knots (288 MPH).

17. **What is the minimum safe altitude that an aircraft may be operated over a congested area of a city?** (14 CFR 91.119)

    Except when necessary for takeoff or landing, no person may operate an aircraft over a congested area of a city, town, or settlement, or over any open-air assembly of persons, below an altitude of 1,000 feet above the highest obstacle within a horizontal radius of 2,000 feet of the aircraft.

18. **In areas other than congested areas, what minimum safe altitudes shall be used?** (14 CFR 91.119)

    Except when necessary for takeoff or landing, an aircraft shall be operated no lower than 500 feet above the surface, except over open water or sparsely populated areas. In those cases, the aircraft may not be operated closer than 500 feet to any person, vessel, vehicle or structure.

19. **Define "minimum safe altitude."** (14 CFR 91.119)

    An altitude allowing, if a power unit fails, an emergency landing without undue hazard to persons or property on the surface.

20. **What is the lowest altitude an aircraft may be operated over an area designated as a U.S. wildlife refuge, park or Forest Service Area?** (AIM 7-4-6)

    All aircraft are requested to maintain a minimum altitude of 2,000 feet above the surface.

21. When flying below 18,000 feet MSL, cruising altitude must be maintained by reference to an altimeter set using what procedure? (14 CFR 91.121)

When the barometric pressure is 31.00" Hg or less, each person operating an aircraft must maintain the cruising altitude of that aircraft by reference to an altimeter that is set to the current reported altimeter setting of a station along the route and within 100 nautical miles of the aircraft. If there is no station within this area, the current reported altimeter setting of an available station may be used. If the barometric pressure exceeds 31.00" Hg, consult the *Aeronautical Information Manual* for correct procedures.

22. If an altimeter setting is not available before flight, what procedure should be used? (14 CFR 91.121)

Use the same procedure as in the case of an aircraft not equipped with a radio: the elevation of the departure airport or an appropriate altimeter setting available before departure should be used.

23. When may a pilot intentionally deviate from an ATC clearance or instruction? (14 CFR 91.123)

No pilot may deviate from an ATC clearance unless:

a. an amended clearance has been obtained,

b. an emergency exists,

c. or in response to a traffic and collision avoidance system resolution advisory.

24. As pilot-in-command, what action, if any, is required of you if you deviate from an ATC instruction and priority is given? (14 CFR 91.123)

Two actions are required of you as PIC:

a. Each pilot-in-command who, in an emergency or in response to a traffic alert and collision avoidance system resolution advisory, deviates from an ATC clearance or instruction must notify ATC of that deviation as soon as possible.

b. Each pilot-in-command who is given priority by ATC in an emergency shall submit a detailed report of that emergency within 48 hours to the manager of that ATC facility, if requested by ATC (on-the-ground responsibility).

25. In the event of radio failure while operating an aircraft to, from, through or on an airport having an operational tower, what are the different types and meanings of light gun signals you might receive from an ATC tower? (14 CFR 91.125)

Light	On Ground	In Air
Steady Green	Cleared for Takeoff	Cleared to Land
Flashing Green	Cleared to Taxi	Return for Landing
Steady Red	Stop	Yield, Continue Circling
Flashing Red	Taxi Clear of Runway	Unsafe, Do Not Land
Flashing White	Return to Start	Not Used
Alternate Red/Green	Exercise Extreme Caution	Exercise Extreme Caution

Note: Most pilots find these hard to remember; always have a reference available in the cockpit (kneeboard, placard, or EFB app).

26. If the aircraft radio fails in flight under VFR while operating into a tower controlled airport, what conditions must be met before a landing may be made at that airport? (14 CFR 91.126, 91.127, 91.129)

a. Weather conditions must be at or above basic VFR weather minimums;

b. Visual contact with the tower is maintained; and

c. A clearance to land is received.

27. What procedures should be used when attempting communications with a tower when the aircraft transmitter or receiver or both are inoperative? (AIM 4-2-13)

Arriving Aircraft Receiver Inoperative:

a. Remain outside or above Class D surface area.

b. Determine direction and flow of traffic.

c. Advise tower of aircraft type, position, altitude, and intention to land. Request to be controlled by light signals.

d. At 3 to 5 miles, advise tower of position and join traffic pattern.

e. Watch tower for light gun signals.

Arriving Aircraft Transmitter Inoperative:

a. Remain outside or above Class D surface area.

b. Determine direction and flow of traffic.

c. Monitor frequency for landing or traffic information.

d. Join the traffic pattern and watch for light gun signals.

e. Daytime, acknowledge by rocking wings. Nighttime, acknowledge by flashing landing light or navigation lights.

Arriving Aircraft Transmitter and Receiver Inoperative:

a. Remain outside or above Class D surface area.

b. Determine direction and flow of traffic.

c. Join the traffic pattern and watch for light gun signals.

d. Acknowledge light signals as noted above.

28. What general rules apply concerning traffic pattern operations at non-tower airports within Class E or G airspace? (14 CFR 91.126, 91.127)

Each person operating an aircraft to or from an airport without an operating control tower shall:

a. in the case of an airplane approaching to land, make all turns of that airplane to the left unless the airport displays approved light signals or visual markings indicating that turns should be made to the right, in which case the pilot shall make all turns to the right.

b. in the case of an aircraft departing an airport, comply with any traffic patterns established for that airport in Part 93.

29. When operating in Class D airspace, what procedure should be used when approaching to land on a runway with a Visual Approach Slope Indicator? (14 CFR 91.129)

Aircraft approaching to land on a runway served by a Visual Approach Slope Indicator shall maintain an altitude at or above the glide slope until a lower altitude is necessary for a safe landing.

30. What is the fuel requirement for VFR flight at night? (14 CFR 91.151)

No person may begin a flight in an airplane under VFR conditions unless (considering wind and forecast weather conditions) there is enough fuel to fly to the first point of intended landing and, assuming normal cruising speed, at night, to fly after that for at least 45 minutes.

31. What is the fuel requirement for VFR flight during the day? (14 CFR 91.151)

During the day, you must be able to fly to the first point of intended landing, and assuming normal cruising speed, to fly after that for at least 30 minutes.

32. When operating an aircraft under VFR in level cruising flight at an altitude of more than 3,000 feet above the surface, what rules apply concerning specific altitudes flown? (14 CFR 91.159)

When operating above 3,000 feet AGL but less than 18,000 feet MSL on a *magnetic course* of 0° to 179°, fly at an odd-thousand-foot MSL altitude plus 500 feet. When on a *magnetic course* of 180° to 359°, fly at an even-thousand-foot MSL altitude plus 500 feet.

33. What is an "ELT"? (AIM 6-2-4)

Emergency Locator Transmitter — A radio transmitter attached to the aircraft structure which operates from its own power source on 121.5, 243.0 MHz, and the newer 406 MHz. It aids in locating downed aircraft by radiating a downward-sweeping audio tone, 2 – 4 times a second. It is designed to function without human action after an accident. It can be operationally tested during the first 5 minutes after any hour. (*Note:* Digital 406 MHz ELTs should only be tested per the manufacturer's instructions.)

34. Is an emergency locator transmitter required on all aircraft? (14 CFR 91.207)

No person may operate a U.S. registered civil airplane unless there is attached to the airplane an automatic-type emergency locator transmitter that is in operable condition. Several exceptions exist, including the following:

a. Aircraft engaged in training operations conducted entirely within a 50-nautical-mile radius of the airport from which such local flight operations began.

b. Aircraft engaged in design and testing.

c. New aircraft engaged in manufacture, preparation and delivery.

d. Aircraft engaged in agricultural operations.

35. When must the batteries in an emergency locator transmitter be replaced or recharged, if rechargeable? (14 CFR 91.207)

Batteries used in ELTs must be replaced (or recharged, if the batteries are rechargeable):

a. When the transmitter has been in use for more than 1 cumulative hour; or

b. When 50 percent of their useful life (or, rechargeable batteries, 50 percent of their useful life of charge), has expired.

Note: The new expiration date for replacing (or recharging) the battery must be legibly marked on the outside of the transmitter and entered in the aircraft maintenance record. This date indicates 50% of the battery's useful life.

36. What are the regulations concerning use of supplemental oxygen on board an aircraft? (14 CFR 91.211)

a. At cabin pressure altitudes above 12,500 feet MSL up to and including 14,000 feet MSL: for that part of the flight at those altitudes that is more than 30 minutes, the required minimum flight crew must be provided with and use supplemental oxygen.

b. At cabin pressure altitudes above 14,000 feet MSL: for the entire flight time at those altitudes, the required flight crew is provided with and uses supplemental oxygen.

c. At cabin pressure altitudes above 15,000 feet MSL: each occupant is provided with supplemental oxygen.

37. According to regulations, where is aerobatic flight of an aircraft not permitted? (14 CFR 91.303)

No person may operate an aircraft in aerobatic flight:

a. Over any congested area of a city, town, or settlement;

b. Over an open air assembly of persons;

c. Within the lateral boundaries of the surface areas of Class B, Class C, Class D, or Class E airspace designated for an airport;

d. Within 4 nautical miles of the center line of a Federal airway;

e. Below an altitude of 1,500 feet above the surface; or

f. When flight visibility is less than 3 statute miles.

38. Define aerobatic flight. (14 CFR 91.303)

For the purposes of this section, aerobatic flight means an intentional maneuver involving an abrupt change in an aircraft's attitude, an abnormal attitude, or abnormal acceleration, not necessary for normal flight.

39. When are parachutes required on board an aircraft? (14 CFR 91.307)

a. Unless each occupant of the aircraft is wearing an approved parachute, no pilot of a civil aircraft carrying any person (other than a crewmember) may execute any intentional maneuver that exceeds:

• a bank angle of 60° relative to the horizon; or

• a nose-up or nose-down attitude of 30° relative to the horizon.

b. The above regulation does not apply to:

• flight tests for pilot certification or rating; or

• spins and other flight maneuvers required by the regulations for any certificate or rating when given by a CFI or ATP instructing in accordance with 14 CFR §61.67.

E. Airspace

Exam Tip: Be prepared to explain the type of airspace your planned route of flight will take you through from departure to arrival at your destination. Know the required visibility, cloud clearance and communication requirements at any point and altitude along your route of flight. Also, expect the "what if you're here" questions concerning special use airspace, special VFR clearances, etc.

1. What is Class A airspace? (AIM 3-2-2)

Generally, that airspace from 18,000 feet MSL up to and including FL600, including that airspace overlying the waters within 12 nautical miles of the coast of the 48 contiguous states and Alaska; and designated international airspace beyond 12 nautical miles of the coast of the 48 contiguous states and Alaska within areas of domestic radio navigational signal or ATC radar coverage, and within which domestic procedures are applied.

2. Can a flight under VFR be conducted within Class A airspace? (14 CFR 91.135)

No, unless otherwise authorized by ATC, each person operating an aircraft in Class A airspace must operate that aircraft under instrument flight rules (IFR).

3. What is the minimum pilot certification for operations conducted within Class A airspace? (14 CFR 91.135)

The pilot must be at least a private pilot with an instrument rating.

4. What minimum equipment is required for flight operations within Class A airspace? (14 CFR 91.135)

a. A two-way radio capable of communicating with ATC on the frequency assigned.

b. A Mode C altitude encoding transponder.

c. Equipped with instruments and equipment required for IFR operations.

5. How is Class A airspace depicted on navigational charts? (AIM 3-2-2)

Class A airspace is not specifically charted.

6. What is the definition of Class B airspace? (AIM 3-2-3)

Generally, that airspace from the surface to 10,000 feet MSL surrounding the nation's busiest airports in terms of IFR operations or passenger enplanements. The configuration of each Class B airspace area is individually tailored and consists of a surface area and two or more layers (some Class B airspace areas resemble upside down wedding cakes), and is designated to contain all published instrument procedures once an aircraft enters the airspace.

7. What minimum pilot certification is required to operate an aircraft within Class B airspace? (14 CFR 91.131)

No person may take off or land a civil aircraft at an airport within a Class B airspace area or operate a civil aircraft within a Class B airspace area unless:

a. The pilot-in-command holds at least a private pilot certificate;

b. The pilot-in-command holds a recreational pilot certificate and has met the requirements of 14 CFR §61.101; or for a student pilot seeking a recreational pilot certificate met the requirements of 14 CFR §61.94.

Continued

c. The pilot-in-command holds a sport pilot certificate and has met the requirements of 14 CFR §61.325; or the requirements for a student pilot seeking a recreational pilot certificate in 14 CFR §61.94.

d. The aircraft is operated by a student pilot who has met the requirements of 14 CFR §61.94 or §61.95 of this chapter, as applicable.

Certain Class B airspace areas do not allow pilot operations to be conducted to or from the primary airport, unless the pilot-in-command holds at least a private pilot certificate (example: Dallas/Fort Worth International).

8. What is the minimum equipment required for operations of an aircraft within Class B airspace? (14 CFR 91.131)

a. An operable two-way radio capable of communications with ATC on the appropriate frequencies for that area.

b. A Mode C altitude encoding transponder.

c. If IFR, an operable VOR or TACAN receiver or an operable and suitable RNAV system.

9. Before operating an aircraft into Class B airspace, what basic requirement must be met? (14 CFR 91.131)

Arriving aircraft must obtain an ATC clearance from the ATC facility having jurisdiction for that area prior to operating an aircraft in that area.

10. What minimum weather conditions are required when conducting VFR flight operations within Class B airspace? (14 CFR 91.155)

VFR flight operations must be conducted clear of clouds with at least 3 statute miles flight visibility.

11. How is Class B airspace depicted on navigational charts? (AIM 3-2-3)

Class B airspace is charted on Sectional Charts, IFR En Route Low Altitude, and Terminal Area Charts. A solid shaded blue line depicts the lateral limits of Class B airspace. Numbers indicate the base and top, i.e. $^{100}/_{25}$, $^{100}/_{SFC}$.

12. What basic ATC services are provided to all aircraft operating within Class B airspace? (AIM 3-2-3)

VFR pilots will be provided sequencing and separation from other aircraft while operating within Class B airspace.

13. It becomes apparent that wake turbulence may be encountered while ATC is providing sequencing and separation services in Class B airspace. Whose responsibility is it to avoid this turbulence? (AIM 3-2-3)

The pilot-in-command is responsible. The services provided by ATC do not relieve pilots of their responsibilities to see and avoid other traffic operating in basic VFR weather conditions, to adjust their operations and flight path as necessary to preclude serious wake turbulence encounters, to maintain appropriate terrain and obstruction clearance, or to remain in weather conditions equal to or better than the minimums required by 14 CFR §91.155.

14. What is the maximum speed allowed when operating inside Class B airspace, under 10,000 feet and within a Class D surface area? (14 CFR 91.117)

Unless otherwise authorized or required by ATC, no person may operate an aircraft at or below 2,500 feet above the surface within 4 nautical miles of the primary airport of a Class C or Class D airspace area at an indicated airspeed of more than 200 knots. This restriction does not apply to operations conducted within a Class B airspace area. Such operations shall comply with the "below 10,000 feet MSL" restriction: "No person shall operate an aircraft below 10,000 feet MSL, at an indicated airspeed of more than 250 knots."

15. When operating beneath the lateral limits of Class B airspace, or in a VFR corridor designated through Class B airspace, what maximum speed is authorized? (14 CFR 91.117)

No person may operate an aircraft in the airspace underlying a Class B airspace area designated for an airport or in a VFR corridor designated through such a Class B airspace area, at an indicated airspeed of more than 200 knots (230 MPH).

16. What is Class C airspace? (AIM 3-2-4)

Generally, that airspace from the surface to 4,000 feet above the airport elevation (charted in MSL) surrounding those airports that have an operational control tower, are serviced by a radar approach control, and that have a certain number of IFR operations or passenger enplanements.

17. What are the basic dimensions of Class C airspace? (AIM 3-2-4)

Although the configuration of each Class C airspace area is individually tailored, the airspace usually consists of a 5 NM radius core surface area that extends from the surface up to 4,000 feet above the airport elevation, and a 10 NM radius shelf area that extends from 1,200 feet to 4,000 feet above the airport elevation. The outer area radius will be 20 NM, with some variations based on site specific requirements. The outer area extends outward from the primary airport and extends from the lower limits of radar/radio coverage up to the ceiling of the approach controls airspace.

18. What minimum pilot certification is required to operate an aircraft within Class C airspace? (AIM 3-2-4)

A student pilot certificate.

19. What minimum equipment is required to operate an aircraft within Class C airspace? (14 CFR 91.130, 91.215)

Unless otherwise authorized by the ATC having jurisdiction over the Class C airspace area, no person may operate an aircraft within a Class C airspace area designated for an airport unless that aircraft is equipped with the following:

a. A two-way radio.

b. Automatic pressure altitude reporting equipment with Mode C capability.

20. When operating an aircraft through Class C airspace or to an airport within Class C airspace, what basic requirement must be met? (14 CFR 91.130)

Each person must establish two-way radio communications with the ATC facilities providing air traffic services prior to entering that airspace and thereafter maintain those communications while within that airspace.

21. Two-way radio communications must be established prior to entering Class C airspace. Define what is meant by "established" in this context. (AIM 3-2-4)

If a controller responds to a radio call with, "(aircraft call sign) standby," radio communications have been established. It is important to understand that if the controller responds to the initial radio call *without* using the aircraft identification, radio communications have *not* been established and the pilot may not enter the Class C airspace.

22. When departing a satellite airport without an operative control tower located within Class C airspace, what requirement must be met? (14 CFR 91.130)

Each person must establish and maintain two-way radio communications with the ATC facilities having jurisdiction over the Class C airspace area as soon as practicable after departing.

23. What minimum weather conditions are required when conducting VFR flight operations within Class C airspace? (14 CFR 91.155)

VFR flight operations within Class C airspace require 3 statute miles flight visibility and cloud clearances of at least 500 feet below, 1,000 feet above and 2,000 feet horizontal to clouds.

24. How is Class C airspace depicted on navigational charts? (AIM 3-2-4)

A solid magenta line is used to depict Class C airspace. Class C airspace is charted on Sectional Charts, IFR En Route Low Altitude, and Terminal Area Charts where appropriate.

25. What type of Air Traffic Control services are provided when operating within Class C airspace? (AIM 3-2-4)

When two-way radio communications and radar contact are established, all VFR aircraft are:

a. Sequenced to the primary airport.

b. Provided Class C services within the Class C airspace and the outer area.

c. Provided basic radar services beyond the outer area on a workload permitting basis. This can be terminated by the controller if workload dictates.

26. Describe the various types of terminal radar services available for VFR aircraft. (AIM 4-1-18)

Basic radar service—Safety alerts, traffic advisories, limited radar vectoring (on a workload-permitting basis) and sequencing at locations where procedures have been established for this purpose and/or when covered by a letter of agreement.

TRSA service—radar sequencing and separation service for VFR aircraft in a TRSA.

Class C service—This service provides, in addition to basic radar service, approved separation between IFR and VFR aircraft, and sequencing of VFR arrivals to the primary airport.

Class B service—Provides, in addition to basic radar service, approved separation of aircraft based on IFR, VFR, and/or weight, and sequencing of VFR arrivals to the primary airport(s).

27. Where is Mode C altitude encoding transponder equipment required? (AIM 4-1-20)

a. At or above 10,000 feet MSL over the 48 contiguous states or the District of Columbia, excluding that airspace below 2,500 feet AGL.

b. Within 30 miles of a Class B airspace primary airport, below 10,000 feet MSL

c. Within and above all Class C airspace, up to 10,000 feet MSL;

d. Within 10 miles of certain designated airports, excluding that airspace which is both outside the Class D surface area and below 1,200 feet AGL.

e. All aircraft flying into, within, or across the contiguous U.S. ADIZ.

Note: Civil and military transponders should be turned to the "on" or normal altitude reporting position prior to moving on the airport surface to ensure the aircraft is visible to ATC surveillance systems.

28. What is the maximum speed an aircraft may be operated within Class C airspace? (AIM 3-2-4)

Unless otherwise authorized or required by ATC, no person may operate an aircraft at or below 2,500 feet above the surface within 4 nautical miles of the primary airport of a Class C airspace area at an indicated speed of more than 200 knots (230 MPH).

29. What is Class D airspace? (AIM 3-2-5)

Generally, Class D airspace extends upward from the surface to 2,500 feet above the airport elevation (charted in MSL) surrounding those airports that have an operational control tower. The configuration of each Class D airspace area is individually tailored and when instrument procedures are published, the airspace will normally be designed to contain those procedures.

30. When operating an aircraft through Class D airspace or to an airport within Class D airspace, what requirement must be met? (14 CFR 91.129)

Each person must establish two-way radio communications with the ATC facilities providing air traffic services prior to entering that airspace and thereafter maintain those communications while within that airspace.

31. When departing a satellite airport without an operative control tower located within Class D airspace, what requirement must be met? (14 CFR 91.129)

Each person must establish and maintain two-way radio communications with the ATC facility having jurisdiction over the Class D airspace area as soon as practicable after departing.

32. Is an ATC clearance required if flight operations are conducted through a Class E surface area arrival extension? (AIM 3-2-5, 3-2-6)

Class E airspace may be designated as extensions to Class B, Class C, Class D, and Class E surface areas. Class E airspace extensions begin at the surface and extend up to the overlying controlled airspace. The extensions provide controlled airspace to contain standard instrument approach procedures without imposing a communications requirement on pilots operating under VFR. Surface area arrival extensions become part of the surface area and are in effect during the same times as the surface area.

33. What minimum weather conditions are required when conducting VFR flight operations within Class D airspace? (14 CFR 91.155)

VFR flight operations within Class D airspace require 3 statute miles flight visibility and cloud clearances of at least 500 feet below, 1,000 feet above and 2,000 feet horizontal to clouds.

34. How is Class D airspace depicted on navigational charts? (AIM 3-2-5)

Class D airspace areas are depicted on Sectional and Terminal charts with blue segmented lines, and on IFR Enroute Lows with a boxed [D].

35. What type of Air Traffic Control services are provided when operating within Class D airspace? (AIM 3-2-5, 5-5-8, and 5-5-10)

No separation services are provided to VFR aircraft. When meteorological conditions permit, regardless of the type of flight plan or whether or not under the control of a radar facility, the pilot is responsible to see and avoid other traffic, terrain or obstacles. A controller, on a workload permitting basis, will provide radar traffic information, safety alerts and traffic information for sequencing purposes.

36. What is the maximum speed an aircraft may be operated within Class D airspace? (AIM 3-2-5)

Unless otherwise authorized or required by ATC, no person may operate an aircraft at or below 2,500 feet above the surface within 4 nautical miles of the primary airport of a Class D airspace area at an indicated airspeed of more than 200 knots (230 MPH).

37. When a control tower, located at an airport within Class D airspace, ceases operation for the day, what happens to the lower limit of the controlled airspace? (AIM 3-2-5)

During the hours the tower is not in operation, Class E surface area rules, or a combination of Class E rules down to 700 feet AGL and Class G rules to the surface, will become applicable. Check the *Chart Supplement U.S.* for specifics.

38. Will all airports with an operating control tower always have Class D airspace surrounding them? (AIM 4-3-2)

No; some airports do not have the required weather reporting capability necessary for surface based controlled airspace. The controlled airspace over these airports normally begins at 700 feet or 1,200 feet AGL and can be determined from visual aeronautical charts.

39. What is the definition of Class E (controlled) airspace? (AIM Glossary)

Controlled airspace is airspace of defined dimensions within which air traffic control service is provided to IFR flights and to VFR flights in accordance with the airspace classification. Controlled airspace is a generic term that covers Class A, Class B, Class C, Class D, and Class E airspace.

40. State several examples of Class E airspace. (AIM 3-2-6)

a. *Surface area designated for an airport where a control tower is not in operation*—Class E surface areas extend upward from the surface to a designated altitude, or to the adjacent or overlying controlled airspace and are configured to contain all instrument procedures.

Continued

b. *Extension to a surface area*—Class E airspace may be designated as extensions to Class B, Class C, Class D, and Class E surface areas. Class E airspace extensions begin at the surface and extend up to the overlying controlled airspace. The extensions provide controlled airspace to contain standard instrument approach procedures without imposing a communications requirement on pilots operating under VFR.

c. *Airspace used for transition*—Class E airspace areas may be designated for transitioning aircraft to/from the terminal or enroute environment. They extend upward from either 700 feet AGL or 1,200 feet AGL and are designated for airports with an approved instrument procedure. The 700-foot/1,200-foot AGL Class E airspace transition areas remain in effect continuously, regardless of airport operating hours or surface area status.

d. *Enroute domestic areas*—Class E airspace areas that extend upward from a specified altitude and provide controlled airspace in those areas where there is a requirement to provide IFR enroute ATC services but the Federal airway system is inadequate.

e. *Federal airways and low-altitude RNAV routes*—Federal airways and low-altitude RNAV routes are Class E airspace areas and, unless otherwise specified, extend upward from 1,200 feet AGL to, but not including 18,000 feet MSL.

f. *Offshore airspace areas*—Class E airspace areas that extend upward from a specified altitude to, but not including 18,000 feet MSL. These areas provide controlled airspace beyond 12 miles from the coast of the U.S. in those areas where there is a requirement to provide IFR enroute ATC services, and within which the U.S. is applying domestic procedures.

g. *Unless designated at a lower altitude*—Class E airspace in the U.S. consists of the airspace extending upward from 14,500 feet MSL to, but not including 18,000 feet MSL overlying the 48 contiguous states, the District of Columbia and Alaska, including the waters within 12 NM from the coast of the 48 contiguous states and Alaska.

h. *The airspace above FL 600 is Class E airspace.*

41. What are the operating rules and pilot/equipment requirements to operate within Class E airspace? (AIM 3-2-6)

a. Minimum pilot certification—student pilot certificate.

b. No specific equipment requirements in Class E airspace.

c. No specific requirements for arrival or through flight in Class E airspace.

42. When a Class C or Class D surface area is not in effect continuously (for example, where a control tower only operates part-time), what will happen to the surface area airspace when the tower closes? (AIM 3-2-6)

The surface area airspace will change to either a Class E surface area or Class G airspace. In such cases, the "Airspace" entry for the airport in the *Chart Supplement U.S.* will state "other times Class E" or "other times Class G." When a part-time surface area changes to Class E airspace, the Class E arrival extensions will remain in effect as Class E airspace. If a part–time Class C, Class D, or Class E surface area becomes Class G airspace, the arrival extensions will change to Class G at the same time.

43. Explain the purpose of Class E transition areas. (AIM 3-2-6)

Class E transition areas extend upward from either 700 feet AGL (magenta vignette) or 1,200 feet AGL (blue vignette) and are designated for airports with an approved instrument procedure. Class E transition areas exist to help separate (via cloud clearance) arriving and departing IFR traffic from VFR aircraft operating in the vicinity.

44. Are you required to establish communications with a tower located within Class E airspace? (14 CFR 91.127)

Yes; unless otherwise authorized or required by ATC, no person may operate an aircraft to, from, through, or on an airport having an operational control tower unless two-way communications are maintained between that aircraft and the control tower. Communications must be established prior to 4 nautical miles from the airport, up to and including 2,500 feet AGL.

45. How is Class E airspace depicted on navigational charts? (AIM 3-2-6; USRGD)

Class E airspace below 14,500 feet MSL is charted on Sectional, Terminal, and IFR Enroute Low Altitude charts. The lateral and vertical limits of all Class E controlled airspace up to but not including 18,000 feet are shown by narrow bands of vignette on Sectional and Terminal Area charts. Controlled airspace floors of 700 feet AGL are defined by a magenta vignette; floors other than 700 feet that abut uncontrolled airspace are defined by a blue vignette; differing floors greater than 700 feet AGL are annotated by a symbol and a number indicating the floor. If the ceiling is less than 18,000 feet MSL, the value (prefixed by the word "ceiling") is shown along the limits of the controlled airspace.

46. How are Class E surface extension areas depicted on navigational charts? (USRGD)

Class E airspace areas that serve as extensions to Class B, Class C, and Class D airspace are depicted by a magenta segmented line.

47. What is the definition of Class G airspace? (AIM 3-3-1)

Class G or uncontrolled airspace is that portion of the airspace that has not been designated as Class A, B, C, D, or E airspace. It is airspace in which air traffic control has no authority or responsibility to control air traffic; however, pilots should remember there are VFR minimums that apply to this airspace.

48. Are you required to establish communications with a tower located within Class G airspace? (14 CFR 91.126)

Yes; unless otherwise authorized or required by ATC, no person may operate an aircraft to, from, through, or on an airport having an operational control tower unless two-way communications are maintained between that aircraft and the control tower. Communications must be established prior to 4 nautical miles from the airport, up to and including 2,500 AGL.

49. What are the vertical limits of Class G airspace? (FAA-H-8083-25)

Class G airspace begins at the surface and continues up to the overlying controlled (Class E) airspace, not to exceed 14,500 feet MSL.

50. What is the minimum cloud clearance and visibility required when conducting flight operations in a traffic pattern at night in Class G airspace below 1,200 feet AGL? (14 CFR 91.155)

When the visibility is less than 3 statute miles but not less than 1 statute mile during night hours, an airplane may be operated clear of clouds if operated in an airport traffic pattern within one-half mile of the runway.

51. What is the main difference between Class G airspace and Class A, B, C, D, and E airspace?

The main difference which distinguishes Class G airspace from Class A, B, C, D, and E airspace is the flight visibility/cloud clearance requirements necessary to operate within it.

52. What minimum flight visibility and clearance from clouds are required for VFR flight in the following situations? (14 CFR 91.155)

Class C, D, or E Airspace

Less than 10,000 feet MSL:
   Visibility: 3 statute miles.
   Cloud clearance: 500 feet below, 1,000 feet above, 2,000 feet horizontal.

At or above 10,000 feet MSL:
   Visibility: 5 statute miles.
   Cloud clearance: 1,000 feet below, 1,000 feet above, 1 statute mile horizontal.

Class G Airspace

1,200 feet or less above the surface (regardless of MSL altitude):
   Day
      Visibility: 1 statute mile.
      Cloud clearance: clear of clouds
   Night
      Visibility: 3 statute miles
      Cloud clearance: 500 feet below, 1,000 feet above, 2,000 feet horizontal.

Continued

More than 1,200 feet above the surface but less than 10,000 ft. MSL:
Day
Visibility: 1 statute mile
Cloud clearance: 500 feet below, 1,000 feet above,
2,000 feet horizontal.

Night
Visibility: 3 statute miles
Cloud clearance: 500 feet below, 1,000 feet above,
2,000 feet horizontal.

More than 1,200 feet above the surface and at or above
10,000 feet MSL:
Visibility: 5 statute miles
Cloud clearance: 1,000 feet below, 1,000 feet above,
1 statute mile horizontal.

53. What are the "basic" VFR weather minimums required for operation of an aircraft into Class B, Class C, Class D, or Class E airspace? (14 CFR 91.155)

1,000-foot ceiling and 3 miles visibility. Except as provided in
14 CFR §91.157 (special VFR), no person may:

a. Operate an aircraft beneath the ceiling under VFR within the lateral boundaries of controlled airspace designated to the surface for an airport when the ceiling is less than 1,000 feet.

b. Take off or land an aircraft, or enter the traffic pattern of an airport, under VFR, within the lateral boundaries of the surface areas of Class B, Class C, Class D, or Class E airspace designated for an airport unless ground visibility at that airport is at least 3 statute miles or, if ground visibility is not reported, unless flight visibility during landing or takeoff, or while operating in the traffic pattern is at least 3 statute miles.

54. If VFR flight minimums cannot be maintained, can a VFR flight be made into Class B, C, D, or E airspace? (AIM 4-4-6)

No, with one exception. A "Special VFR clearance" may be obtained from ATC prior to operating within a Class B, Class C, Class D, or Class E surface area provided the flight can remain clear of clouds with at least one statute mile ground visibility if taking off or landing or, one statute mile flight visibility for operations within Class B, Class C, Class D, and Class E surface areas.

55. Are Special VFR clearances always available to pilots in all classes of airspace? (AIM 4-4-6)

A VFR pilot may request and be given a clearance to enter, leave, or operate within most Class D and Class E surface areas and some Class B and Class C surface areas traffic permitting and providing such flight will not delay IFR operations.

Note: Special VFR operations by fixed wing aircraft are prohibited in some Class B and Class C surface areas due to the volume of IFR traffic. A list of these Class B and Class C surface areas is contained in 14 CFR Part 91. They are also depicted on Sectional Aeronautical Charts.

56. If it becomes apparent that a special VFR clearance will be necessary, what facility should the pilot contact in order to obtain one? (AIM 4-4-6)

When a control tower is located within a Class B, Class C, or Class D surface area, requests for clearances should be made to the tower. In a Class E surface area, a clearance may be obtained from the nearest tower, FSS, or center.

57. Can a "Special VFR clearance" be obtained into or out of Class B, C, D, or E airspace at night? (AIM 4-4-6)

Special VFR operations by fixed-wing aircraft are prohibited between sunset and sunrise unless the pilot is instrument rated and the aircraft is equipped for IFR flight.

58. What is a "Prohibited Area"? (AIM 3-4-2)

Prohibited areas contain certain airspace of defined dimensions identified by an area on the surface of the earth within which the flight of aircraft is prohibited. Such areas are established for security or other reasons associated with the national welfare.

59. What is a "Restricted Area"? (AIM 3-4-3)

Restricted areas contain airspace identified by an area on the surface of the earth within which the flight of aircraft, while not wholly prohibited, is subject to restrictions. These areas denote the existence of unusual, often invisible, hazards to aircraft such as artillery firing, aerial gunnery, or guided missiles. Penetration of restricted areas without authorization from the using or controlling agency may be extremely hazardous to the aircraft and its occupants.

60. Under what conditions, if any, may pilots enter restricted or prohibited areas? (14 CFR 91.133)

No person may operate an aircraft within a restricted area contrary to the restrictions imposed, or within a prohibited area, unless that person has the permission of the using or controlling agency. Normally *no* operations are permitted within a prohibited area and *prior* permission must always be obtained before operating within a restricted area.

61. What is a "Warning Area"? (AIM 3-4-4)

A warning area is airspace of defined dimensions extending from three nautical miles outward from the coast of the United States, containing activity that may be hazardous to nonparticipating aircraft. The purpose of such an area is to warn nonparticipating pilots of the potential danger. A warning area may be located over domestic or international waters, or both.

62. What is a "MOA"? (AIM 3-4-5)

A Military Operating Area (MOA) consists of airspace of defined vertical and lateral limits established for the purpose of separating certain military training activities from IFR traffic. Pilots operating under VFR should exercise extreme caution while flying within an MOA when military activity is being conducted. The activity status (active/inactive) of MOAs may change frequently. Therefore, pilots should contact any FSS within 100 miles of the area to obtain accurate real-time information concerning the MOA hours of operation. Prior to entering an active MOA, pilots should contact the controlling agency for traffic advisories.

63. What is an "Alert Area"? (AIM 3-4-6)

Alert areas are depicted on aeronautical charts to inform nonparticipating pilots of areas that may contain a high volume of pilot training or an unusual type of aerial activity. Pilots should be particularly alert when flying in these areas. All activity within an Alert Area shall be conducted in accordance with regulations, without waiver, and pilots of participating aircraft as well as pilots transiting the area shall be equally responsible for collision avoidance.

64. What are "Controlled Firing Areas"? (AIM 3-4-7)

Controlled Firing Areas (CFAs) contain activities that, if not conducted in a controlled environment, could be hazardous to nonparticipating aircraft. The distinguishing feature of the CFA, as compared to other special use airspace, is that its activities are suspended immediately when spotter aircraft, radar or ground lookout positions indicate an aircraft might be approaching the area. CFAs are not charted.

65. What is a "National Security Area"? (AIM 3-4-8)

National Security Areas consist of airspace of defined vertical and lateral dimensions established at locations where there is a requirement for increased security and safety of ground facilities. Pilots are requested to voluntarily avoid flying through the depicted NSA. When is it necessary to provide a greater level of security and safety, flight in NSAs may be temporarily prohibited by regulation under the provisions of 14 CFR §99.7.

66. What is a Special Flight Rules Area (SFRA)? (14 CFR Part 93)

An SFRA is an area of airspace within which Special Federal Aviation Regulations (SFARs) apply. Examples include the Washington D.C. SFRA and the Grand Canyon SFRA. Established operating requirements and procedures to operate within the SFRA can be found in 14 CFR Part 93 and on the specific chart legend for that area. Always check NOTAMs for possible procedural changes in the SFRA.

67. Where can information on special use airspace be found? (AIM 3-4-1)

Special use airspace (except CFAs) are charted on IFR or visual charts and include the hours of operation, altitudes, and the controlling agency. (Additional information may be found at **https://sua.faa.gov**.)

68. Where can a pilot find information on VFR flyways, VFR Corridors, and Class B airspace transition routes used to transition busy terminal airspace? (AIM 3-5-5)

Information will normally be depicted on the reverse side of VFR Terminal Area Charts, commonly referred to as Class B airspace charts.

69. What are "Military Training Routes"? (AIM 3-5-2)

Military Training Routes are developed for use by the military for the purpose of conducting low-altitude, high speed training. The routes above 1,500 feet AGL are developed to be flown, to the maximum extent possible, under IFR. The routes at 1,500 feet AGL and below are generally developed to be flown under VFR. Routes below 1,500 feet AGL use four-digit identifiers (i.e. IR 1004, VR 1008). Routes above 1,500 feet AGL use three-digit identifiers, (i.e. IR 003, VR 004). IR is for IFR routes and VR is for VFR routes.

70. What is a "TRSA"? (AIM Glossary)

A Terminal Radar Service Area (TRSA) consists of airspace surrounding designated airports wherein ATC provides radar vectoring, sequencing, and separation on a full time basis for all IFR and participating VFR aircraft. Pilot participation is urged but not mandatory.

71. What class of airspace is a "TRSA"? (AIM 3-5-6)

TRSAs do not fit into any of the U.S. airspace classes and are not contained in 14 CFR Part 71 nor are there any operating rules in Part 91. The primary airport(s) within the TRSA become Class D airspace. The remaining portion of a TRSA overlies other controlled airspace which is normally Class E airspace beginning at 700 or 1,200 feet and established to transition to/from the enroute/terminal environment. TRSAs will continue to be an airspace area where participating pilots can receive additional radar services which have been redefined as TRSA service.

72. How are TRSAs depicted on navigational charts?
(AIM 3-5-6)

TRSAs are depicted on VFR sectional and terminal area charts with a solid black line and altitudes for each segment. The Class D portion is charted with a blue segmented line.

73. What are ADIZ and where are they located? (AIM Glossary)

An Air Defense Identification Zone is an area of airspace over land or water, extending upward from the surface, within which the ready identification, the location and the control of aircraft are required in the interest of national security. ADIZ locations are:

Domestic—located within U.S. along an international boundary.

Coastal—located over coastal waters of the U.S.

Distant Early Warning Identification Zone (DEWIZ)—located over coastal waters of the State of Alaska.

Land-based ADIZ—located over U.S. metropolitan areas.

74. What requirements must be satisfied prior to operations into, within or across an ADIZ? (AIM 5-6-1)

Operational requirements for aircraft operations associated with an ADIZ are as follows:

Flight plan—An IFR or DVFR flight plan must be filed with the appropriate aeronautical facility.

Two-way radio—An operating two-way radio is required.

Transponder—Aircraft must be equipped with an operable radar beacon transponder having altitude reporting (Mode C) capabilities. The transponder must be turned on and set to the assigned ATC code.

Position reports—For IFR flights, normal position reporting. For DVFR flights, an estimated time of ADIZ penetration must be filed at least 15 minutes prior to entry.

Continued

Aircraft position tolerances—Over land, a tolerance of ±5 minutes from the estimated time over a reporting point and within 10 NM from the centerline of an intended track over an estimated reporting point. Over water, a tolerance of ±5 minutes from the estimated time over a reporting point or point of penetration and within 20 NM from centerline of an intended track over an estimated reporting point.

Land-based ADIZ—are activated and deactivated over U.S. metropolitan areas as needed, with dimensions, activation dates, etc., disseminated via NOTAM. In addition to other ADIZ requirements, pilots must report landing or leaving the land-based ADIZ if flying too low for radar coverage.

F. Airspace Classification Summary

The following section summarizes the requirements for operations within the various airspace classes.

1. Discuss "Class A" airspace.

Vertical dimensions....... 18,000 feet MSL up to and include FL600
Operations permitted ....IFR
Entry prerequisites.. ATC Clearance
Minimum pilot qualifications .... Instrument rating
Two-way radio communications.. Yes
VFR minimum visibility...N/A
VFR minimum distance from clouds..N/A
Aircraft separation ....All
Conflict resolution ....N/A
Traffic advisories ....N/A
Safety advisories.. Yes

2. Discuss "Class B" airspace.

Vertical dimensions.............................. Surface to 10,000 feet MSL
Operations permitted .... IFR and VFR
Entry prerequisites.. ATC clearance
Minimum pilot qualifications .... Private/Student
Two-way radio communications.. Yes
VFR Minimum visibility ....3 statute miles
VFR Minimum distance from clouds ....Clear of clouds
Aircraft separation ....All
Conflict resolution .... Yes

Traffic advisories .... Yes
Safety advisories.. Yes

3. Discuss "Class C" airspace.

Vertical dimensions........ Surface to 4,000 feet AGL (charted MSL)
Operations permitted .... IFR and VFR
Entry prerequisites...... ATC clearance for IFR; radio contact for all
Minimum pilot qualifications .... Student certificate
Two-way radio communications.. Yes
VFR Minimum visibility ....3 statute miles
VFR Minimum distance from clouds .... 500' below, 1,000' above,
and 2,000' horizontal
Aircraft separation .... IFR, SVFR and runway operations
Conflict resolution ....Between IFR and VFR operations
Traffic advisories .... Yes
Safety advisories.. Yes

4. Discuss "Class D" airspace.

Vertical dimensions........ Surface to 2,500 feet AGL (charted MSL)
Operations permitted .... IFR and VFR
Entry prerequisites...... ATC clearance for IFR; radio contact for all
Minimum pilot qualifications .... Student certificate
Two-way radio communications.. Yes
VFR Minimum visibility ....3 statute miles
VFR Minimum distance from clouds .... 500' below, 1,000' above,
and 2,000' horizontal
Aircraft separation .... IFR, SVFR and runway operations
Conflict resolution .... No
Traffic advisories ....Workload permitting
Safety advisories.. Yes

5. Discuss "Class E" airspace.

Vertical dimensions: Except for 18,000 feet MSL, no defined vertical limit. Extends upward from either the surface or a designated
altitude to the overlying or adjacent controlled airspace.

Operations permitted .... IFR and VFR
Entry prerequisites....................................... ATC clearance for IFR
Minimum pilot qualifications .... Student certificate
Two-way radio communications................................... Yes for IFR
VFR minimum visibility..*3 statute miles

Continued

VFR minimum distance from clouds..............................*500' below,
1,000' above, and 2,000' horizontal
Aircraft separation ....IFR and SVFR
Conflict resolution ....No
Traffic advisories ....Workload permitting
Safety advisories.. Yes

*Different visibility minima and distance cloud requirements exist
for operations above 10,000 feet MSL and Special VFR.*

6. Discuss "Class G" airspace.

Vertical dimensions............... Surface up to the overlying controlled
(Class E) airspace, not to exceed 14,500 feet MSL
Operations permitted ....IFR and VFR
Entry prerequisites.. None
Minimum pilot qualifications ....Student certificate
Two-way radio communications...No
VFR minimum visibility.. *1 statute mile
VFR minimum distance from clouds....... *500' below, 1,000' above
and 2,000' horizontal
Aircraft separation .... None
Conflict resolution ....No
Traffic advisories ....Workload permitting
Safety advisories.. Yes

*Different visibility minima and distance from cloud requirements
exist for night operations, operations above 10,000 feet MSL, and
operations below 1,200 feet AGL.*

G. National Transportation Safety Board

1. When is immediate notification to the NTSB required?
(NTSB Part 830.5)

The operator of an aircraft shall immediately, and by the most
expeditious means available, notify the nearest NTSB office when
an aircraft accident or any of the following listed serious incidents
occur:

a. Flight control system malfunction

b. Crewmember unable to perform normal duties

c. Inflight fire

d. Aircraft collision inflight

e. Property damage, other than aircraft, estimated to exceed $25,000

f. Overdue aircraft (believed to be in accident)

g. Release of all or a portion of a propeller blade from an aircraft

h. Complete loss of information (excluding flickering), from more than 50 percent of an aircraft's EFIS cockpit displays.

2. Define "aircraft incident." (NTSB Part 830.2)

An aircraft incident means an occurrence other than an accident associated with the operation of an aircraft, which affects or could affect the safety of operations.

3. Define "aircraft accident." (NTSB Part 830.2)

An aircraft accident means an occurrence associated with the operation of an aircraft which takes place between the time any person boards the aircraft with the intention of flight and all such persons have disembarked, and in which any person suffers death or serious injury, or in which the aircraft receives substantial damage.

4. Define the term "serious injury." (NTSB Part 830.2)

Serious injury means any injury that:

a. Requires hospitalization for more than 48 hours, commencing within 7 days from the date the injury was received;

b. Results in a fracture of any bone (except simple fractures of fingers, toes or nose);

c. Causes severe hemorrhages, nerve, muscle or tendon damage;

d. Involves any internal organ; or

e. Involves second- or third-degree burns affecting more than 5% of the body surface.

5. Define the term "substantial damage." (NTSB Part 830.2)

"Substantial damage" means damage or failure which adversely affects the structural strength, performance or flight characteristics of the aircraft and which would normally require major repair or replacement of the affected component. Engine failure or damage limited to an engine if only one engine fails or is damaged; bent

Continued

fairings or cowling; dented skin; small punctured holes in the skin or fabric; ground damage to rotor or propeller blades; and damage to landing gear, wheels, tires, flaps, engine accessories, brakes, or wing tips are not considered substantial damage for the purpose of this part.

6. Will notification to the NTSB always be necessary in any aircraft "accident" even if there were no injuries? (NTSB Part 830)

Refer to the definition of "Accident." An aircraft accident can involve substantial damage and/or injuries, and the NTSB always requires a report if this is the case.

7. Where are accident or incident reports filed? (NTSB Part 830)

The operator of an aircraft shall file any report with the field office of the Board nearest the accident or incident. The National Transportation Safety Board field offices are listed in the U.S. government pages of telephone directories in major cities.

8. After an accident or incident has occurred, how soon must a report be filed with the NTSB? (NTSB Part 830)

The operator shall file a report on NTSB Form 6120.1/2, available from NTSB field offices, the NTSB in Washington D.C., or the FAA Flight Standards District Office:

a. Within 10 days after an accident;

b. When, after 7 days, an overdue aircraft is still missing.

Note: A report on an "Incident" for which notification is required as described shall be filed only as requested by an authorized representative of the NTSB.

9. Can the FAA use reports submitted to NASA for enforcement purposes? (14 CFR 91.25; AC 00-46)

The FAA will not use reports submitted to NASA under the Aviation Safety Reporting Program (or information derived therefrom) in any enforcement action except information concerning accidents or criminal offenses which are wholly excluded from the program. By submitting a report within 10 days following an incident, the pilot is not protected from the FAA finding a violation of regulation, but may be providing himself some immunity from a civil penalty or possible suspension of certificate.

H. Aeronautical Information Manual

1. What type of aeronautical lighting is "VASI"? (AIM 2-1-2)

Visual Approach Slope Indicator (VASI) is a system of lights so arranged to provide visual descent guidance information during the approach to a runway. The basic principle of VASI is that of color differential between red and white: each light projects a beam of light having a white segment in the upper half and a red segment in the lower part of the beam. The lights in a two-bar VASI will be as follows:

Red Over Red — below Glide Path

Red Over White — on Glide Path

White Over White — above Glide Path

2. What is "PAPI"? (AIM 2-1-2)

The Precision Approach Path Indicator (PAPI) uses light units similar to the VASI, but are installed in a single row of either two- or four-light units. These systems have an effective visual range of about 5 miles during the day and up to 20 miles at night. The row of light units are normally installed on the left side of the runway.

Four white lights ....High (More than 3.5 degrees)

Three white one red .... Slightly high (3.2 degrees)

Two white two red .... On glide path (3 degrees)

One white three red................................Slightly low (2.8 degrees)

Four red lights.....................................Low (Less than 2.5 degrees)

3. What does the operation of an airport rotating beacon during the hours of daylight indicate? (AIM 2-1-10)

In Class B, Class C, Class D, and Class E surface areas, operation of the airport beacon during the hours of daylight often indicates that the ground visibility is less than 3 miles and/or the ceiling is

Continued

less than 1,000 feet. ATC clearance in accordance with 14 CFR Part 91 is required for landing, takeoff and flight in the traffic pattern. Pilots should not rely solely on the operation of the airport beacon to indicate if weather conditions are IFR or VFR. There is no regulatory requirement for daylight operation and it is the pilot's responsibility to comply with proper preflight planning as required by 14 CFR Part 91.

4. What are the six types of signs installed at airports?
(AIM 2-3-8 through 2-3-13)

a. *Mandatory instruction sign*—red background/white inscription; denotes an entrance to a runway, a critical area, or a prohibited area.

b. *Location sign*—black background/yellow inscription/yellow border; do not have arrows; used to identify a taxiway or runway location, the boundary of the runway, or identify an ILS critical area.

c. *Direction sign*—yellow background/black inscription; identifies the designation of the intersecting taxiway(s) leading out of an intersection that a pilot would expect to turn onto or hold short of.

d. *Destination sign*—yellow background/black inscription and also contain arrows; provides information on locating runways, terminals, cargo areas, and civil aviation areas, etc.

e. *Information sign*—yellow background/black inscription; used to provide the pilot with information on areas that can't be seen from the control tower, applicable radio frequencies, and noise abatement procedures, etc.

f. *Runway distance remaining sign*—black background/white numeral inscription; indicates the distance of the remaining runway in thousands of feet.

5. What color are runway markings? Taxiway markings?
(AIM 2-3-1)

Markings for runways are white. Markings for taxiways, areas not intended for use by aircraft (closed and hazardous areas), and holding positions (even if they are on a runway) are yellow.

6. What airport marking aids will be used to indicate the following? (AIM 2-3-3, 2-3-5, 2-3-6)

Runway Threshold Markings — These come in two configurations. They either consist of eight longitudinal stripes of uniform dimensions disposed symmetrically about the runway centerline, or the number of stripes is related to the runway width. A threshold marking helps identify the beginning of the runway available for landing.

Displaced Threshold — A threshold located at a point on the runway other than the designated beginning of the runway. A displaced threshold reduces the length of runway available for landings. The portion of runway behind a displaced threshold is available for takeoffs in either direction. A ten-foot wide white threshold bar is located across the width of the runway at the displaced threshold. White arrows are located along the centerline in the area between the beginning of the runway and displaced threshold. White arrowheads are located across the width of the runway just prior to the threshold bar.

Runway Hold Position Markings — For taxiways, these markings indicate where an aircraft is supposed to stop when it does not have clearance to proceed onto the runway. They are also installed on runways only if the runway is normally used by air traffic control for "land, hold short" operations. They consist of four yellow lines, two solid and two dashed, spaced six inches apart and extending across the width of the taxiway or runway.

Temporarily closed runways and taxiways — Provides a visual indication to pilots that a runway/taxiway is temporarily closed. Yellow crosses are placed on the runway only at each end of the runway. Closed taxiways are blocked with barricades or may utilize a yellow cross at the entrance to the taxiway.

Permanently closed runways and taxiways — For runways and taxiways which are permanently closed, the lighting circuits will be disconnected. The runway threshold, runway designation, and touchdown markings are obliterated and yellow crosses are placed at each end of the runway and at 1,000-foot intervals.

7. What are the different methods a pilot may use to determine the proper runway and traffic pattern in use at an airport without an operating control tower? (AIM 4-1-9, 4-3-4)

a. At an airport with a full or part-time UNICOM station in operation, an advisory may be obtained which will usually include wind direction and velocity, favored or designated runway, right or left traffic, altimeter setting, known traffic, NOTAMs, etc.

b. Many airports are now providing completely automated weather, radio check capability and airport advisory information on an automated UNICOM system. Availability of the automated UNICOM will be published in the Chart Supplement U.S. and approach charts.

c. At those airports where these services are not available, a segmented circle visual indicator system, if installed, is designated to provide traffic pattern information. The segmented circle system consists of the following components:

- The segmented circle
- The wind direction indicator (wind sock, cone, or tee)
- The landing direction indicator (a tetrahedron)
- Landing strip indicators
- Traffic pattern indicators

8. What is the standard direction of turns when approaching an uncontrolled airport for landing? (AIM 4-3-3)

When approaching for landing, all turns must be made to the left unless a traffic pattern indicator indicates that turns should be made to the right.

9. What is considered standard for traffic pattern altitude? (AIM 4-3-3)

Unless otherwise established, 1,000 feet AGL is the recommended traffic pattern altitude. At most airports and military air bases, traffic pattern altitudes for propeller-driven aircraft generally extend from 600 feet to as high as 1,500 feet AGL. Also, traffic pattern altitudes for military turbojet aircraft sometimes extend up to 2,500 feet AGL.

10. **What recommended entry and departure procedures should be used at airports without an operating control tower?** (AIM 4-3-3)

    A pilot should plan to enter the traffic pattern in level flight, abeam the midpoint of the runway at pattern altitude. When departing a traffic pattern, continue straight out, or exit with a 45-degree turn (to the left when in a left-hand traffic pattern; to the right when in a right-hand traffic pattern) beyond the departure end of the runway, after reaching pattern altitude.

11. **If in doubt about the traffic pattern altitude for a particular airport, what publication can provide this information?**

    The *Chart Supplement U.S.*

12. **What is an "ARTCC," and what useful service can it provide to VFR flights?** (AIM Glossary)

    An "Air Route Traffic Control Center" is a facility established to provide air traffic control service primarily to aircraft operating on IFR flight plans within controlled airspace and principally during the en route phase of flight. Air Route Surveillance Radar allows them the capability to detect and display an aircraft's position while en route between terminal areas. When equipment capabilities and controller workload permit, certain advisory/assistance service may be provided to VFR aircraft (VFR Flight Following). Frequencies may be obtained from FSS or the *Chart Supplement U.S.* Also, IFR enroute charts have ARTCC sector frequencies depicted. If departing from an airport with a control tower, you can request the appropriate frequency from them.

13. **What are the following transponder codes?**
    (AIM 4-1-20, 6-4-2)

    1200 — VFR operations
    7500 — Hijack
    7600 — Communications failure
    7700 — Emergency

14. When conducting flight operations into an airport with an operating control tower, when should initial contact be established? (AIM 4-3-2)

When operating at an airport where traffic control is being exercised by a control tower, pilots are required to maintain two-way radio contact with the tower while operating within Class B, Class C, and Class D surface areas, unless the tower authorizes otherwise. Initial call-up should be made about 15 miles from the airport. Also, not all airports with an operating control tower will have Class D airspace. These airports do not have weather reporting, which is a requirement for surface-based controlled airspace. Pilots are expected to use good operating practices and communicate with the control tower.

15. What communication procedures are recommended when departing a Class D airspace area? (AIM 4-3-2)

Unless there is good reason to leave the tower frequency before exiting the Class B, Class C and Class D surface areas, it is good operating practice to remain on the tower frequency for the purpose of receiving traffic information. In the interest of reducing tower frequency congestion, pilots are reminded that it is not necessary to request permission to leave the tower frequency once outside of Class B, Class C, and Class D surface areas.

16. How do you convert from standard time to coordinated universal time? (AIM 4-2-12)

You should take the local time (converted to military time) and add the time differential to convert to UTC.

Eastern Standard Time.................... add 5 hours
Central Standard Time .... add 6 hours
Mountain Standard Time .... add 7 hours
Pacific Standard Time..................... add 8 hours
Alaska Standard Time..................... add 9 hours
Hawaii Standard Time .... add 10 hours

Note: For Daylight Savings Time subtract 1 hour from above.

17. Arrange the radio facilities listed below in the order they would be used when operating into or out of a tower controlled airport within Class B, C, or D airspace.

Approach Control

ATIS

Ground Control

Control Tower

Clearance Delivery

Departure Control

Arriving Aircraft: ATIS, Approach Control, Control Tower, Ground Control

Departing Aircraft: ATIS, Clearance Delivery (if required for the surrounding airspace, i.e., Class B, C or D airspace), Ground Control, Control Tower, Departure Control.

18. What are "NOTAMs"? (AIM 5-1-3)

Notices To Airmen (NOTAM)—time-critical aeronautical information of either a temporary nature, or not known sufficiently in advance to permit publication on aeronautical charts or in other operational publications, receives immediate dissemination via the National NOTAM System. This is aeronautical information that could affect a pilot's decision to make a flight. It includes such information as airport or primary runway closures, changes in the status of navigational aids, ILS's, radar service availability, and other information essential to planned en route, terminal, or landing operations. NOTAMs can be viewed via the PilotWeb site: **https://pilotweb.nas.faa.gov/PilotWeb/**

19. What are the five categories of NOTAMs? (AIM 5-1-3)

NOTAMs are classified into five categories:

a. *(D) NOTAMs*—Information that requires wide dissemination via telecommunication and pertains to en route navigational aids, civil public-use airports listed in the AFD, facilities, services, and procedures.

Continued

    b. *FDC NOTAMs*—Flight information that is regulatory in nature including, but not limited to, changes to IFR charts, procedures, and airspace usage.

    c. *POINTER NOTAMs*—issued by a flight service station to highlight or point out another NOTAM; such as an FDC NOTAM. These NOTAMs assist users in cross-referencing important information that may not be found under an airport or NAVAID identifier.

    d. *SAA NOTAMs*—are issued when Special Activity Airspace will be active outside the published schedule times and when required by the published schedule.

    e. *MILITARY NOTAMs*—pertain to U.S. Air Force, Army, Marine, and Navy navigational aids/airports that are part of the NAS.

20. All (D) NOTAMS will have keywords contained within the first part of the text. What are several examples of these keywords? (AIM 5-1-3)

RWY, TWY, RAMP, APRON, AD, OBST, NAV, COM, SVC, AIRSPACE, (U) unverified, (O) other

21. What is a "TFR"? (AC 91-63)

A temporary flight restriction (TFR) is a regulatory action issued via the U.S. NOTAM system to restrict certain aircraft from operating within a defined area, on a temporary basis, to protect persons or property in the air or on the ground. They may be issued due to a hazardous condition, a special event, or as a general warning for the entire FAA airspace. TFR information can be obtained from an AFSS or on the Internet at www.faa.gov.

Exam Tip: On the day of your practical test, verify that a last minute TFR hasn't been issued for your area or along your planned route of flight.

22. Where can NOTAM information be obtained? (AIM 5-1-3)

    a. Flight Service Station

    b. Notice to Airman Publication (NTAP)—printed NOTAMs

    c. DUATs vendors

    d. Internet website—www.faa.gov/pilots/flt_plan/notams/

e. Broadcast Flight Information Services (FIS-B)—displayed in cockpit

23. When are VFR flight plans required to be filed? (AIM 5-1-4)

Except for operations in or penetrating a Coastal or Domestic ADIZ or DEWIZ, a flight plan is not required for VFR flight; however, it is strongly recommended that one be filed with an FAA FSS when making extended cross-country flights. This will ensure that you receive VFR Search and Rescue Protection.

24. What is a DVFR flight plan? (AIM 5-1-6)

Defense VFR; VFR flights into a Coastal or Domestic ADIZ/DEWIZ are required to file VFR flight plans for security purposes. The flight plan must be filed before departure.

25. When you land at an airport with an ATC tower in operation will the tower automatically close your flight plan? (AIM 5-1-14)

Control towers do not automatically close VFR or DVFR flight plans since they do not know if a particular VFR aircraft is on a flight plan. A pilot is responsible for ensuring that his/her VFR or DVFR flight plan is canceled. You should close your flight plan with the nearest FSS, or if one is not available, you may request any ATC facility to relay your cancellation.

26. If your flight is behind schedule, and you do not report the delay, or you forget to close your flight plan, how much time from ETA does the FSS allow before search and rescue efforts are begun? (AIM 5-1-14)

If you fail to report or cancel your flight plan within one-half hour after your ETA, Search and Rescue procedures are started.

27. What is wake turbulence? (AIM Glossary)

A phenomenon resulting from the passage of an aircraft through the atmosphere. The term includes vortices, thrust stream turbulence, jet blast, jet wash, propeller wash, and rotor wash, both on the ground and in the air.

28. Where are wake turbulence and wingtip vortices likely to occur? (AIM 7-3-3)

All aircraft generate turbulence and associated wingtip vortices. In general, avoid the area behind and below the generating aircraft, especially at low altitudes. Also of concern is the weight, speed, and shape of the wing of the generating aircraft. The greatest vortex strength occurs when the generating aircraft is HEAVY, CLEAN and SLOW.

29. What operational procedures should be followed when wake vortices are suspected to exist? (AIM 7-3-6)

a. *Landing behind a larger aircraft on the same runway*—Stay at or above the larger aircraft's final approach flight path. Note its touchdown point and land beyond it.

b. *Landing behind a larger aircraft, when parallel runway is closer than 2,500 feet*—Consider possible drift to your runway. Stay at or above the larger aircraft's final approach flight path, and note its touchdown point.

c. *Landing behind a larger aircraft, crossing runway*—Cross above the larger aircraft's flight path.

d. *Landing behind a departing larger aircraft on the same runway*—Note the larger aircraft's rotation point, and land well prior to rotation point.

e. *Landing behind a departing larger aircraft, crossing runway*—Note the larger aircraft's rotation point. If past the intersection, continue the approach, and land prior to the intersection. If larger aircraft rotates prior to the intersection, avoid flight below the larger aircraft's flightpath. Abandon the approach unless a landing is ensured well before reaching the intersection.

f. *Departing behind a large aircraft*—Note the larger aircraft's rotation point and rotate prior to the larger aircraft's rotation point. Continue climbing above the larger aircraft's climb path until turning clear of the larger aircraft's wake. Avoid subsequent headings that will cross below and behind a larger aircraft.

g. *Intersection takeoffs, same runway*—Be alert to adjacent larger aircraft operations, especially of your runway. If intersection takeoff clearance is received, avoid subsequent heading which will cross below a larger aircraft's path.

h. *Departing or landing after a larger aircraft executing a low approach, missed approach or touch-and-go landing*—Vortices settle and move laterally near the ground. Because of this, the vortex hazard may exist along the runway and in your flight path after a larger aircraft has executed a low approach, missed approach or a touch-and-go landing, particularly in light quartering wind conditions. You should ensure that an interval of at least 2 minutes has elapsed before your takeoff or landing.

i. *En route VFR (thousand-foot altitude plus 500 feet)*—Avoid flight below and behind a large aircraft's path. If a larger aircraft is observed above or on the same track (meeting or overtaking) adjust your position laterally, preferably upwind.

Remember: Acceptance of instructions from ATC is an acknowledgment that the pilot will ensure safe takeoff and landing intervals and accept the responsibility for providing wake turbulence separation.

30. What are several examples of illusions that may lead to landing errors? (AIM 8-1-5)

Runway width illusion—A narrower-than-usual runway can create the illusion that the aircraft is at a higher altitude than it actually is. The pilot who does not recognize this illusion will fly a lower approach, with the risk of striking objects along the approach path or landing short. A wider-than-usual runway can have the opposite effect, with the risk of leveling out high and landing hard or overshooting the runway.

Runway and terrain slopes illusion—An upsloping runway, upsloping terrain, or both, can create the illusion that the aircraft is at a higher altitude than it actually is. The pilot who does not recognize this illusion will fly a lower approach. A downsloping runway, downsloping approach terrain, or both, can have the opposite effect.

Featureless terrain illusion—An absence of ground features, as when landing over water, darkened areas, and terrain made featureless by snow, can create the illusion that the aircraft is at a higher altitude than it actually is. The pilot who does not recognize this illusion will fly a lower approach.

Continued

Atmospheric illusions—Rain on the windscreen can create the illusion of greater height, and atmospheric haze can create the illusion of being at a greater distance from the runway. The pilot who does not recognize these illusions will fly a lower approach.

31. The acronym "LAHSO" refers to what specific air traffic control procedure? (AIM 4-3-11)

LAHSO is an acronym for "land and hold short operations." At controlled airports, ATC may clear a pilot to land and hold short of an intersecting runway, an intersecting taxiway, or some other designated point on a runway. Pilots may accept such a clearance provided that the pilot-in-command determines the aircraft can safely land and stop within the available landing distance (ALD). Student pilots or pilots not familiar with LAHSO should not participate in the program. Pilots are expected to decline a LAHSO clearance if they determine it will compromise safety or if weather is below basic VFR conditions (a minimum ceiling of 1,000 feet and 3 SM visibility).

32. Where can available landing distance (ALD) data be found? (AIM 4-3-11)

ALD data are published in the special notices section of the *Chart Supplement U.S.* and in the U.S. Terminal Procedures Publications. Controllers will also provide ALD data upon request.

33. Discuss recommended collision avoidance procedures and considerations in the following situations. (AIM 4-4-15)

a. *Before takeoff*—Prior to taxiing onto a runway or landing area in preparation for takeoff, pilots should scan the approach area for possible landing traffic, executing appropriate maneuvers to provide a clear view of the approach areas.

b. *Climbs and descents*—During climbs and descents in flight conditions that permit visual detection of other traffic, pilots should execute gentle banks left and right at a frequency that allows continuous visual scanning of the airspace.

c. *Straight and level*—During sustained periods of straight-and-level flight, a pilot should execute appropriate clearing procedures at periodic intervals.

d. *Traffic patterns*—Entries into traffic patterns while descending should be avoided.

e. *Traffic at VOR sites*—Due to converging traffic, sustained vigilance should be maintained in the vicinity of VORs and intersections.

f. *Training operations*—Vigilance should be maintained and clearing turns should be made prior to a practice maneuver. During instruction, the pilot should be asked to verbalize the clearing procedures (call out clear "left, right, above, and below"). High-wing and low-wing aircraft have their respective blind spots. High-wing aircraft should momentarily raise the wing in the direction of the intended turn and look for traffic prior to commencing the turn. Low-wing aircraft should momentarily lower the wing.

34. Where should you look for drones in your area?
(14 CFR Part 107, AIM 7-5-5)

Unmanned aircraft systems (UAS, also called "drones") cannot operate in controlled airspace without obtaining a waiver from the FAA. However, it is possible I might see drones in my area. Drones must fly below 400 feet AGL, can only operate in daylight hours, and must stay clear of clouds.

I. Runway Incursion Avoidance

1. What are three major areas that contribute to runway incursions? (FAA-H-8083-3)

a. *Communications*—misunderstanding the given clearance; failure to communicate effectively

b. *Airport knowledge*—failure to navigate the airport correctly; unable to interpret airport signage

c. *Cockpit procedures for maintaining orientation*—failure to maintain situational awareness

2. **Preflight planning for taxi operations should be an integral part of the pilot's flight planning process. What information should this include?** (AC 91-73)

   a. Review and understand airport signage, markings and lighting.

   b. Review the airport diagram, planned taxi route, and identify any "hot spots."

   c. Review the latest airfield NOTAMs and ATIS (if available) for taxiway/runway closures, construction activity, etc.

   d. Conduct a pre-taxi/pre-landing briefing that includes the expected/assigned taxi route and any hold short lines and restrictions based on ATIS information or previous experience at the airport.

   e. Plan for critical times and locations on the taxi route (complex intersections, crossing runways, etc.).

   f. Plan to complete as many aircraft checklist items as possible prior to taxi.

3. **What is an airport "hot spot"?** (FAA-H-8083-16)

   A "hot spot" is a runway safety-related problem area or intersection on an airport. Typically, hot spots are complex or confusing taxiway–taxiway or taxiway–runway intersections. A lack of visibility may exist at certain points and/or the tower may be unable to see those particular intersections. Pilots should be increasingly vigilant when approaching and taxiing through these intersections.

4. **Why is use of "sterile cockpit" procedures important when conducting taxi operations?** (AC 91-73)

   Pilots must be able to focus on their duties without being distracted by non-flight-related matters unrelated to the safe and proper operation of the aircraft. Refraining from nonessential activities during ground operations is essential. Passengers should be briefed on the importance of minimizing conversations and questions during taxi as well as on arrival, from the time landing preparations begin until the aircraft is safely parked.

5. **When should a pilot request "progressive" taxi instructions?** (AIM 4-3-18)

   If the pilot is unfamiliar with the airport or for any reason confusion exists as to the correct taxi routing, a request may be made for progressive taxi instructions, which include step-by-step routing directions.

6. **After completing your pre-taxi/pre-landing briefing of the taxi route you "expect" to receive, ATC calls and gives you a different route. What potential pitfall is common in this situation?** (AC 91-73)

   A common pitfall of pre-taxi and pre-landing planning is setting expectations and then receiving different instructions from ATC. Pilots need to follow the instructions that they actually receive, and not the ones they expect to receive. Short term memory is of limited duration.

7. **Why is it a good idea to write down taxi instructions, especially at larger or unfamiliar airports?** (AC 91-73)

   Writing down taxi instructions, especially complex instructions, can reduce a pilot's vulnerability to forgetting part of the instructions and provides a reference for read-back of instructions to ATC. It can also be used as a means of reconfirming the taxi route and any restrictions at any time during taxi operations.

8. **When issued taxi instructions to an assigned takeoff runway, are you automatically authorized to cross any runway that intersects your taxi route?** (AIM 4-3-18)

   No; Aircraft must receive a runway crossing clearance for each runway that their taxi route crosses. When assigned a takeoff runway, ATC will first specify the runway, issue taxi instructions, and state any hold short instructions or runway crossing clearances if the taxi route will cross a runway. When issuing taxi instructions to any point other than an assigned takeoff runway, ATC will specify the point to which to taxi, issue taxi instructions, and state any hold short instructions or runway crossing clearances if the taxi route will cross a runway. ATC is required to obtain a read back from the pilot of all runway hold short instructions.

9. **When receiving taxi instructions from a controller, pilots should always read back what information?** (AIM 4-3-18)

   a. The runway assignment.

   b. Any clearance to enter a specific runway.

   c. Any instruction to hold short of a specific runway or line up and wait.

10. **What are some recommended practices that can assist a pilot in maintaining situational awareness during taxi operations?** (AC 91-73)

    a. A current airport diagram should be available for immediate reference during taxi.

    b. Monitor ATC instructions/clearances issued to other aircraft for the "big picture."

    c. Focus attention outside the cockpit while taxiing.

    d. Use all available resources (airport diagrams, airport signs, markings, lighting, and ATC) to keep the aircraft on its assigned taxi route.

    e. Cross-reference heading indicator to ensure turns are being made in the correct direction and that you're on the assigned taxi route.

    f. Prior to crossing any hold short line, visually check for conflicting traffic; verbalize "clear left, clear right."

    g. Be alert for other aircraft with similar call signs on the frequency.

    h. Understand and follow all ATC instructions and if in doubt—Ask!

11. **How can a pilot use aircraft exterior lighting to enhance situational awareness and safety during airport surface operations?** (AC 91-73; SAFO)

    To the extent possible and consistent with aircraft equipment, operating limitations, and pilot procedures, pilots should illuminate exterior lights as follows:

    a. *Engines running*—Turn on the rotating beacon whenever an engine is running.

b. *Taxiing*—Prior to commencing taxi, turn on navigation/position lights and anti-collision lights.

c. *Crossing a runway*—All exterior lights should be illuminated when crossing a runway.

d. *Entering the departure runway for takeoff*—All exterior lights (except landing lights) should be on to make your aircraft more conspicuous to aircraft on final and ATC.

e. *Cleared for takeoff*—All exterior lights, including takeoff/landing lights should be on.

Note: If you see an aircraft in takeoff position on a runway with landing lights ON, that aircraft has most likely received its takeoff clearance and will be departing immediately.

12. **During calm or nearly calm wind conditions, at an airport without an operating control tower, a pilot should be aware of what potentially hazardous situations?** (AC 91-73)

Aircraft may be landing and/or taking off on more than one runway at the airport. Also, aircraft may be using an instrument approach procedure to runways other than the runway in use for VFR operations. The instrument approach runway may intersect the VFR runway. It is also possible that an instrument arrival may be made to the opposite end of the runway from which a takeoff is being made.

13. **You have just landed at a tower-controlled airport and missed your assigned taxiway for exiting the runway. Is it permissible for you to turn around on the runway and return to the exit taxiway?** (AIM 4-3-20)

No; At airports with an operating control tower, pilots should never stop or reverse course on the runway without first obtaining ATC approval.

14. **When taxiing at a non-towered airport, what are several precautionary measures you should take prior to entering or crossing a runway?** (AC 91-73)

    Listen on the appropriate frequency (CTAF) for inbound aircraft information and always scan the full length of the runway, including the final approach and departure paths, before entering or crossing the runway. Self-announce your position and intentions and remember that not all aircraft are radio-equipped.

15. **ATC has instructed you to line up and wait on the departure runway due to crossing traffic on an intersecting taxiway. What is considered a reasonable amount of time to wait for a takeoff clearance before calling ATC?** (AIM 5-2-4; SAFO 11004)

    FAA analysis of accidents and incidents involving aircraft holding in position indicate that two minutes or more elapsed between the time the instruction was issued to line up and wait and the resulting event (for example, land-over or go-around). If you have been holding in position on the runway for more than 90 seconds, or you see or hear a potential conflict, contact ATC immediately.

J. Aviation Security

1. **What are several actions you can take to enhance aircraft security?** (TSA)

    a. Always lock your aircraft.

    b. Keep track of door/ignition keys and don't leave keys in unattended aircraft.

    c. Use secondary locks (prop, tie down, throttle, and wheel locks) or aircraft disabler if available.

    d. Lock hangar when unattended.

2. What type of airport security procedures should you review regularly to prevent unauthorized access to aircraft at your airport? (FSSAT)

a. Limitations on ramp access to people other than instructors and students

b. Standards for securing aircraft on the ramp

c. Securing access to aircraft keys at all times

d. New auxiliary security items for aircraft (prop locks, throttle locks, locking tie downs)

e. After-hours or weekend access procedures

3. Give some examples of what you would consider suspicious activity at an airport. (TSA)

a. Aircraft with unusual modifications (such as modified N-numbers) or activity

b. Unfamiliar persons loitering for extended periods in the vicinity of parked aircraft

c. Anyone making threats

d. Events or circumstances that do not fit the pattern of lawful, normal activity at an airport

e. Pilots appearing to be under the control of others

4. When witnessing suspicious or criminal activity, what are three basic ways for reporting the suspected activity? (TSA)

If you determine that it's safe, question the individual. If their response is unsatisfactory and they continue to act suspiciously:

a. Alert airport or FBO management.

b. Contact local law enforcement if the activity poses an immediate threat to persons or property.

c. Contact the 866-GA-SECURE hotline to document the reported event.

5. What is the purpose of the 866-GA-SECURE phone number? (TSA)

866-GA-SECURE is a toll-free hotline operated by the Transportation Security Administration (TSA) Security Operations Center. It is staffed 24/7 to take reports of suspicious or criminal activity occurring at general aviation airports. TSA personnel will document the reported activity, collect your personal contact numbers, and pass the information on to the appropriate regulatory office within the TSA.

Note: Calling 866-GA-SECURE will not dispatch local law enforcement. In the event of an immediate emergency, 911 or local law enforcement should be contacted first.

6. What are several sources of information available to pilots interested in additional guidance on aviation security? (TSA; FSSAT)

Security Guidelines for General Aviation Airports is a set of federally endorsed guidelines that offers an extensive list of options, ideas, and suggestions for the airport operator, sponsor, tenant and/ or user to choose from when considering security enhancements for GA facilities.

Flight School Security Awareness Training for Aircraft and Simulators is an online training course designed to raise the general security awareness levels of employees working in the flight training industry.

Additional Study Questions

1. Prior to departure, what items should you brief your passengers on? (FAA-H-8083-3)

2. When navigating by VOR, when will you have "reverse sensing?" (FAA-H-8083-25)

3. If your Mode C transponder fails while en route, can you continue flight into Class B or Class C airspace? (AIM 4-1-20)

4. Is a mode C transponder required for flight over Class C airspace if operating below 10,000 ft. MSL? (AIM 4-1-20)

5. During preflight planning and while en route, how can pilots mitigate the risk involved with deteriorating weather conditions at their destination? (FAA-H-8083-2)

6. Where can a pilot find information on the location of the nearest VOT testing station? (AIM 1-1-4)

7. Discuss the various factors a pilot should consider when making a Go/No-Go decision for a particular flight. (FAA-H-8083-25)

8. How will you position your aircraft's flight control surfaces while taxiing in the following conditions: quartering tailwind, quartering headwind? (FAA-H-8083-3)

9. Demonstrate the following hand signals utilized by a lineman when directing you to or from a ramp: (AIM 4-3-25)

   a. All clear (OK)

   b. Start engine

   c. Pull chocks

   d. Come ahead

Continued

  e. **Left turn**

  f. **Right turn**

  g. **Slow down**

  h. **Stop**

  i. **Insert chocks**

  j. **Cut engines**

  k. **Emergency stop**

10. **What two factors should be considered when evaluating the type of survival equipment to carry for a flight over uninhabited terrain?** (AIM 6-2-6)

11. **Why is a postflight inspection recommended, and what are you looking for during that inspection?** (FAA-H-8083-3)

12. **Why do the Class E airspace cloud clearance and visibility requirements change above 10,000 feet?** (FAA Safety ALC-25)

Night
Operations

7

A. Night Preparation

1. Name the two distinct types of light-sensitive cells located in the retina of the eye. (FAA-H-8083-3)

Rods and cones are the light-sensitive cells located in the retina.

2. What is the function of the cones, and where are they located in the eye? (FAA-H-8083-3)

The cones are used to detect color, detail and far-away objects and are located in the center of the retina at the back of the eye. They are less sensitive to light, require higher levels of intensity to become active, and are most useful in the daylight hours.

3. What is the function of the rods, and where are they located in the eye? (FAA-H-8083-3)

Rods are located in the back of the eye or retina. The rods function when something is seen out of the corner of the eye or peripheral vision. They detect objects, particularly those that are moving, but do not give detail or color—only shades of gray. Both the cones and the rods are used for vision during daylight. In the absence of normal light, the process of night vision is placed almost entirely on the rods.

4. What is the average time it takes for the rods and cones to become adapted to darkness? (FAA-H-8083-3)

The cones will take approximately 5 to 10 minutes to become adjusted to darkness. Much more time—about 30 minutes—is needed for the rods to become adjusted to darkness.

5. What should the pilot do to accommodate changing light conditions? (FAA-H-8083-3)

The pilot should allow enough time for the eyes to become adapted to the low light levels, and then should avoid exposure to bright light which could cause temporary blindness.

6. **Give several examples of illusions related to ground lighting conditions.** (FAA-H-8083-3)

   a. On a clear night, distant stationary lights can be mistaken for stars or other aircraft. Certain geometrical patterns of ground lights, such as a freeway, runway, approach, or even lights on a moving train can cause confusion. Dark nights tend to eliminate reference to a visual horizon.

   b. A black-hole approach occurs when the landing is made from over water or non-lighted terrain where the runway lights are the only source of light. Without peripheral visual cues to help, pilots will have trouble orientating themselves relative to Earth. The runway can seem out of position (downsloping or upsloping) and in the worse case, results in landing short of the runway.

   c. Night landings can be complicated by the difficulty of judging distance and the possibility of confusing approach and runway lights. For example, when a double row of approach lights joins the boundary lights of the runway, there can be confusion where the approach lights terminate and runway lights begin. Under certain conditions, approach lights can make the aircraft seem higher in a turn to final, than when its wings are level.

7. **During takeoff you suddenly feel as if the aircraft is in an excessively high nose-up attitude. What type of illusion is this?** (AIM 8-1-5)

   Somatogravic illusion. A rapid acceleration during takeoff can create the illusion of being in a nose up attitude. A pilot disoriented by a somatogravic illusion may respond by pushing the aircraft into a nose low, or dive attitude.

8. **When approaching a well-lit runway surrounded by a dark area with little or no features, what illusion should a pilot be alert for?** (AIM 8-1-5)

   Featureless terrain illusion—an absence of ground features, as when landing over water, darkened areas, and terrain made featureless by snow, can create the illusion that the aircraft is at a higher altitude than it actually is. The pilot who does not recognize this illusion will fly a lower approach.

9. What should the pilot do to maintain good eyesight? (FAA-H-8083-3)

Good eyesight depends upon physical condition. Fatigue, colds, vitamin deficiency, alcohol, stimulants, smoking, or medication can seriously impair vision.

10. What can the pilot do to improve the effectiveness of vision at night? (FAA-H-8083-3)

a. Adapt the eyes to darkness prior to flight and keep them adapted. About 30 minutes is needed to adjust after exposure to a bright light.

b. If oxygen is available, use it during night flying. Significant deterioration in night vision can occur at cabin altitudes as low as 5,000 feet.

c. Close one eye when exposed to bright light to help avoid the blinding effect.

d. Do not wear sunglasses after sunset.

e. Move the eyes more slowly than in daylight.

f. Blink the eyes if they become blurred.

g. Concentrate on seeing objects.

h. Force the eyes to view off center.

i. Maintain good physical condition.

j. Avoid smoking, drinking, and using drugs that may be harmful.

11. What equipment should the pilot have for night flight operations? (FAA-H-8083-3)

At least one reliable flashlight is recommended as standard equipment on all night flights. A reliable incandescent or light-emitting diode (LED) flashlight able to produce white/red light and blue for chart reading is preferable. Include a second flashlight (such as a head-mounted type) as a backup. The white light is used while performing the preflight visual inspection, and the red light is used when performing cockpit operations. A spare set of batteries is also recommended.

12. What other items should the pilot have on board for night flights? (FAA-H-8083-3)

Aeronautical charts are essential for night cross-country flight and, if the intended course is near the edge of the chart, the adjacent chart should also be available. It is also recommended to have a spare set of batteries for the flashlight readily available. Organize equipment and charts and place them within easy reach prior to taxiing.

13. Explain the arrangement and interpretation of the position lights on an aircraft. (FAA-H-8083-3)

A red light is positioned on the left wingtip, a green light on the right wingtip, and a white light on the tail. If both a red and green light of another aircraft are observed, and the red light is on the left and the green to the right, the airplane is flying in the same direction. Care must be taken not to overtake the other aircraft and to maintain clearance. If red were on the right and green to the left, the airplane could be on a collision course.

14. Position lights are required to be on during what period of time? (14 CFR 91.209)

From sunset to sunrise.

15. When an aircraft is operated in, or in close proximity to, a night operations area, what is required of an aircraft? (14 CFR 91.209)

The aircraft must:

a. be clearly illuminated,

b. have lighted position lights, or

c. be in an area which is marked by obstruction lights.

16. Are aircraft anticollision lights required to be on during night flight operations? (14 CFR 91.209)

Yes; however, the anticollision lights need not be lighted when the pilot-in-command determines that, because of operating conditions, it would be in the interest of safety to turn the lights off.

17. What are Runway End Identifier Lights (REIL)?
(AIM 2-1-3)

REILs are installed at many airfields to provide rapid and positive identification of the approach end of a particular runway. The system consists of a pair of synchronized flashing lights located laterally on each side of the runway threshold. REILs may be omnidirectional or unidirectional facing the approach area.

18. Describe a Runway Edge Light System. (AIM 2-1-4)

Runway edge lights are used to outline the edges of runways during periods of darkness or restricted visibility conditions. They are white, except on instrument runways yellow replaces white on the last 2,000 feet or half the runway length, whichever is less, to form a caution zone for landings. The lights marking the ends of the runway emit red light toward the runway to indicate the end of runway to a departing aircraft and emit green outward from the runway end to indicate the threshold to landing aircraft. These light systems are classified according to the intensity or brightness they are capable of producing. Examples are: High Intensity Runway Lights (HIRL), Medium Intensity Runway Lights (MIRL), and the Low Intensity Runway Lights (LIRL).

19. Describe a Runway Centerline Lighting System (RCLS).
(AIM 2-1-5)

Runway centerline lights—installed on some precision approach runways to facilitate landing under adverse visibility conditions. They are located along the runway centerline and are spaced at 50-foot intervals. When viewed from the landing threshold, the runway centerline lights are white until the last 3,000 feet of the runway. The white lights begin to alternate with red for the next 2,000 feet, and for the last 1,000 feet of the runway, all centerline lights are red.

20. What are Touchdown Zone Lights (TDZL)? (AIM 2-1-5)

Touchdown zone lights consist of two rows of transverse light bars disposed symmetrically about the runway centerline. The system consists of steady-burning white lights which start at 100 feet beyond the landing threshold and extend to 3,000 feet beyond the landing threshold or to the midpoint of the runway, whichever is less.

21. Describe several different types of taxiway lighting. (AIM 2-1-11)

a. *Taxiway edge lights* — outline the edges of taxiways; consist of blue lights.

b. *Taxiway centerline lights* — assists ground traffic in low visibility conditions; consists of steady-burning green lights.

c. *Clearance bar lights* — installed at holding positions on taxiways; consist of three in-pavement steady-burning yellow lights.

d. *Runway guard lights* — installed at taxiway/runway intersections; consists of either a pair of elevated flashing lights on either side of taxiway or in-pavement yellow lights installed across the taxiway.

e. *Stop bar lights* — used to confirm ATC clearance to enter or cross an active runway in low visibility conditions; consists of a row of red, unidirectional, steady-burning in-pavement lights installed across the taxiway and a pair of elevated steady burning red lights on each side.

22. What are the different types of rotating beacons used to identify airports? (AIM 2-1-10)

White and green	Lighted land airport
Green alone*	Lighted land airport
White & yellow	Lighted water airport
Yellow alone*	Lighted water airport
Green, yellow & white	Lighted heliport
White (dual peaked & green)	Lighted military airport

*Green alone or yellow alone is used only in connection with a white and green or white and yellow beacon display respectively.

23. Describe several types of obstruction lighting.
(AIM 2-2-3)

a. *Aviation red obstruction lights* — flashing aviation red beacons and steady burning aviation red lights during nighttime operations.

b. *Medium and high intensity white obstruction lights* — may be used during daytime and twilight with reduced intensity for nighttime operation. Not normally installed on structures less than 200 feet.

c. *Dual lighting* — a combination of flashing aviation red beacons and steady-burning aviation red lights for nighttime operations and flashing high intensity white lights for daytime operation.

d. *Catenary lighting* — medium and high intensity flashing white markers for high voltage transmission lines and support structures.

24. How does a pilot determine the status of a light system at a particular airport? (FAA-H-8083-3)

The pilot needs to check the *Chart Supplement U.S.* and any Notices to Airmen (NOTAMs) to find out about available lighting systems, light intensities and radio-controlled light system frequencies.

Exam Tip: Be prepared to determine and explain the type and status of airport and runway lighting at your departure and destination airports.

25. How does a pilot activate a radio-controlled runway light system while airborne? (AIM 2-1-9)

The pilot activates radio-controlled lights by keying the microphone on a specified frequency. The following sequence can be used for typical radio controlled lighting systems:

a. On initial arrival, key the microphone seven times to turn the lights on and achieve maximum brightness.

b. If the runway lights are already on upon arrival repeat the above sequence to ensure a full 15 minutes of lighting.

c. The intensity of the lights can be adjusted by keying the microphone seven, five, or three times within 5 seconds.

B. Night Flight

1. During preflight what things should be done to adequately prepare for the night flight? (FAA-H-8083-3)

a. Study all weather reports and forecasts. Particular attention should be directed towards temperature/dewpoint spreads to detect the possibility of fog formation.

b. Calculate wind directions and speeds along the proposed route of flight to ensure accurate drift calculations, as night visual perception of drift is generally inaccurate.

c. Obtain applicable aeronautical charts for both the proposed route as well as adjacent charts, and mark lighted checkpoints clearly.

d. Review all radio navigational aids for correct frequencies and availability.

e. If a GPS is being used for navigation, ensure that it is working properly before the flight. All necessary waypoints should be loaded properly before the flight and the database should be checked for accuracy prior to taking off, and then checked again once in flight.

f. Check all personal equipment such as flashlights and portable transceivers for proper operation.

g. The aircraft should be thoroughly preflighted.

h. All aircraft position lights, as well as the landing light and rotating beacon, should be checked for proper operation.

i. Ground areas should be checked for obstructions that may not be readily visible from within the cockpit.

2. What are some guidelines to follow during the starting, taxiing, and run-up phases of a night flight? (FAA-H-8083-3)

a. The pilot should exercise extra caution on "clearing" the propeller arc area. The use of lights prior to and after engine startup can also alert persons in the area to the presence of the active aircraft.

b. During taxiing, avoid unnecessary use of electrical equipment which would put an abnormal load on the electrical system, such as the landing light. Additionally, other pilots taxiing in the area can be blinded by your landing light or strobes, so avoid using them during taxiing.

c. Taxi slowly and follow any taxi lines.

3. What are some of the guidelines to follow during takeoff and departure phases of a night flight? (FAA-H-8083-3)

a. During takeoff the pilot should:

- on the initial takeoff roll, use both the distant runway edge lights as well as the landing light area to keep the aircraft straight and parallel in the runway, and

- upon liftoff, keep a positive climb by referencing the attitude indicator along with positive rate of climb on the vertical speed indicator.

b. During climbout:

- do not initiate any turns until reaching safe maneuvering altitude, and

- turn the landing light off after climb.

4. What should the pilot do to provide proper orientation and navigation during a night flight? (FAA-H-8083-3)

a. Exercise caution to avoid flying into clouds or a layer of fog. Usually, the first indication of flying into restricted visibility conditions is the gradual disappearance of lights on the ground. If the lights begin to take on an appearance of being surrounded by a halo or glow, use caution in attempting further flight in that same direction, as this is indicative of ground fog.

b. Practice and acquire competency in straight-and-level flight, climbs and descents, level turns, climbing and descending turns, and steep turns. Recovery from unusual attitudes should also be practiced, but only on dual flights with a flight instructor.

Continued

c. Practice the above maneuvers with all the cockpit lights turned OFF—this type of "blackout" training will prove helpful later on, in the event of an electrical or instrument light failure. Include the use of the navigation equipment and local NAVAIDs in this exercise.

d. Continually monitor position, time estimates, and fuel consumed. NAVAIDs, if available, should be used to assist in monitoring enroute progress.

5. If an engine failure occurs at night, what procedures should be followed? (FAA-H-8083-3)

If the engine fails at night, the same procedures apply for dealing with the situation in the daytime. Maintain positive control of the airplane—do not panic. A normal glide should be established and maintained and the airplane turned toward an airport or away from congested areas. A check should be made to determine the cause of the engine failure, such as position of the magnetos, fuel selectors, or primer. If unsuccessful in restart procedures, select 7700 on the transponder and 121.5 on your radio. Declare an emergency, stating WHO you are, WHERE you are, and WHAT your intentions are. In some cases, where radar is available (Approach Control, Center, etc.) you may obtain a quick vector to the nearest airport if within gliding distance. If you have done your homework, you planned your route of flight within gliding distance of lighted airports. If not, two possibilities exist for emergency landing areas:

Lighted areas—interstate highways, roads, parking lots, etc. Advantages include being able to see where and what you are landing on, and having a relatively improved surface to land upon. Disadvantages include all kinds of obstructions to deal with, such as wires, poles, traffic, etc.

Unlighted areas—dark areas with relatively few lights indicating an open area such as a field, lake, etc. Advantages include few or no obstructions to deal with. Disadvantages include not being able to see what you have selected to land on until illumination by your landing light, and the higher possibility that what you have selected is unimproved, rough terrain, etc. As nearly as possible, land into the wind, with flaps, at minimum approach speed. Complete a prelanding checklist, and immediately before touchdown, secure all systems (electrical, fuel) and open the doors.

Whatever your decision, maintain positive control of the aircraft all the way down. A controlled crash will always be more survivable than an uncontrolled crash.

6. **What procedures should be followed during the approach and landing phase of a night flight?**
(FAA-H-8083-3)

   a. The pilot should identify the airport and associated airport lighting and runway lighting.

   b. The aircraft should be flown towards the airport beacon until the runway lights are identified.

   c. A powered approach should be used because visual perception during a descent at night can be difficult.

   d. The landing light should be switched on upon entering the airport traffic area.

   e. The pilot should avoid the use of excessive speed on approach and landing.

Additional Study Questions

1. What is good operating practice concerning the use of aircraft lighting (taxi, landing, strobes) while on the ground at night? (FAA-H-8083-3)

2. Why is it especially important to maintain an organized cockpit when flying at night? (FAA-H-8083-3)

3. When conducting an airplane preflight inspection for a local night flight, in addition to those involved in all flights, what are some general items that you should include? (FAA-H-8083-3)

4. When flying VFR at night, in addition to flying an altitude appropriate for the direction of flight, what else can a pilot do to minimize risk? (AIM 5-1-2)

5. Discuss the various types of cockpit and exterior lighting equipment installed in your airplane. (FAA-H-8083-3)

6. What procedure should be utilized when attempting to land at night without a landing light? (FAA-H-8083-3)

7. Why is it especially important pilots be current in basic attitude instrument flying procedures when flying at night? (FAA-H-8083-3)

8. During the enroute segment of a night flight, how can a pilot determine they are flying from VFR conditions to potentially marginal VFR or IFR conditions? (FAA-H-8083-3)

9. When planning a night flight (local or X/C), what weather information should be particularly significant to the pilot? (FAA-H-8083-3)

10. Discuss your method of route and checkpoint selection, when planning a night VFR cross-country flight. (FAA-H-8083-3)

Human Factors 8

A. Flight Physiology

1. What is hypoxia? (AIM 8-1-2)

Hypoxia is a state of oxygen deficiency in the body sufficient to impair functions of the brain and other organs.

2. Where does hypoxia usually occur, and what symptoms should one expect? (AIM 8-1-2)

Although a deterioration in night vision occurs at a cabin pressure altitude as low as 5,000 feet, other significant effects of altitude hypoxia usually do not occur in the normal healthy pilot below 12,000 feet. From 12,000 feet to 15,000 feet of altitude, judgment, memory, alertness, coordination, and ability to make calculations are impaired, and headache, drowsiness, dizziness and either a sense of well-being or belligerence occur. Effects are worse above 15,000 feet.

3. What factors can make a pilot more susceptible to hypoxia? (AIM 8-1-2)

The altitude at which significant effects of hypoxia occur can be lowered by a number of factors. Carbon monoxide inhaled in smoking or from exhaust fumes, lowered hemoglobin (anemia), and certain medications can reduce the oxygen-carrying capacity of the blood. Small amounts of alcohol and low doses of certain drugs, such as antihistamines, tranquilizers, sedatives, and analgesics can, through their depressant action, render the brain much more susceptible to hypoxia. Extreme heat and cold, fever, and anxiety increase the body's demand for oxygen, and hence its susceptibility to hypoxia.

4. How can hypoxia be avoided? (AIM 8-1-2)

Hypoxia is prevented by heeding factors that reduce tolerance to altitude, by enriching the inspired air with oxygen from an appropriate oxygen system, and by maintaining a comfortable, safe cabin pressure altitude. For optimum protection, pilots are encouraged to use supplemental oxygen above 10,000 feet during the day, and above 5,000 feet at night.

5. What is hyperventilation? (AIM 8-1-3)

Hyperventilation, or an abnormal increase in the volume of air breathed in and out of the lungs, can occur subconsciously when a stressful situation is encountered in flight. This results in a significant decrease in the carbon dioxide content of the blood. Carbon dioxide is needed to automatically regulate the breathing process.

6. What symptoms can a pilot expect from hyperventilation? (AIM 8-1-3)

As hyperventilation "blows off" excessive carbon dioxide from the body, a pilot can experience symptoms of light-headedness, suffocation, drowsiness, tingling in the extremities, and coolness, and react to them with even greater hyperventilation. Incapacitation can eventually result from uncoordination, disorientation, and painful muscle spasms. Finally, unconsciousness can occur.

7. How can a hyperventilating condition be reversed? (AIM 8-1-3)

The symptoms of hyperventilation subside within a few minutes after the rate and depth of breathing are consciously brought back to normal. The buildup of carbon dioxide in the body can be hastened by controlled breathing in and out of a paper bag held over the nose and mouth.

8. What is carbon monoxide poisoning? (AIM 8-1-4)

Carbon monoxide is a colorless, odorless and tasteless gas contained in exhaust fumes. When inhaled, even in minute quantities over a period of time, it can significantly reduce the ability of the blood to carry oxygen. Consequently, effects of hypoxia occur.

9. How does carbon monoxide poisoning occur, and what symptoms should a pilot be alert for? (AIM 8-1-4)

Most heaters in light aircraft work by air flowing over the manifold. The use of these heaters while exhaust fumes are escaping through manifold cracks and seals is responsible every year for several nonfatal and fatal aircraft accidents from carbon monoxide poisoning. A pilot who detects the odor of exhaust or experiences symptoms of headache, drowsiness, or dizziness while using the heater should suspect carbon monoxide poisoning.

10. What action should be taken if a pilot suspects carbon monoxide poisoning? (AIM 8-1-4)

A pilot who suspects this condition to exist should immediately shut off the heater and open all air vents. If symptoms are severe, or continue after landing, medical treatment should be sought.

11. What is the cause of motion sickness, and what are its symptoms? (FAA-H-8083-25)

Motion sickness is caused by continued stimulation of the inner ear, which controls the sense of balance. The symptoms are progressive and include loss of appetite, saliva collecting in the mouth, perspiration, nausea, disorientation, headaches, and possible vomiting. The pilot may become incapacitated if it becomes severe enough.

12. What action should be taken if a pilot or his passenger suffers from motion sickness? (FAA-H-8083-25)

If suffering from airsickness while piloting an aircraft, open up the air vents, loosen the clothing, use supplemental oxygen, and keep the eyes on a point outside the airplane. Avoid unnecessary head movements. Terminate the flight and land as soon as possible.

13. What is "ear block"? (AIM 8-1-2)

As the aircraft cabin pressure decreases during ascent, the expanding air in the middle ear pushes the Eustachian tube open. The air then escapes down to the nasal passages and equalizes in pressure with the cabin pressure. But during descent, the pilot must periodically open the Eustachian tube to equalize pressure. Either an upper respiratory infection, such as a cold or sore throat, or a nasal allergic condition can produce enough congestion around the Eustachian tube to make equalization difficult. Consequently, the difference in pressure between the middle ear and aircraft cabin can build to a level that will hold the Eustachian tube closed, making equalization difficult if not impossible. An ear block produces severe pain and loss of hearing that can last from several hours to several days.

14. **What action can be taken to prevent ear block from occurring in flight?** (AIM 8-1-2)

Normally this can be accomplished by swallowing, yawning, tensing muscles in the throat or, if these do not work, by the combination of closing the mouth, pinching the nose closed and attempting to blow through the nostrils (Valsalva maneuver). It is also prevented by not flying with an upper respiratory infection or nasal allergic condition.

15. **What regulations apply and what common sense should prevail concerning the use of alcohol?** (14 CFR 91.17, AIM 8-1-1)

The regulations prohibit pilots from performing crewmember duties within 8 hours after drinking any alcoholic beverage, while under the influence of alcohol, or having .04 percent weight or more alcohol in the blood. Due to the slow destruction of alcohol in the bloodstream, a pilot may still be under influence, or over the .04 percent mark, 8 hours after drinking a moderate amount of alcohol. Therefore, an excellent rule is to allow at least 12 to 24 hours from "bottle to throttle," depending on the amount of alcoholic beverage consumed.

16. **For a pilot who has been taking an over-the-counter (OTC) cold medication, how do the various environmental factors the pilot is exposed to inflight affect the drug's physiological impact on the pilot?** (FAA-H-8083-25)

Drugs that cause no apparent side effects on the ground can create serious problems at relatively low altitudes. Even at typical general aviation altitudes, the changes in concentrations of atmospheric gases in the blood can enhance the effects of seemingly innocuous drugs and result in impaired judgment, decision-making, and performance.

17. **What regulations apply and what common sense should prevail concerning the use of drugs and medication?** (AIM 8-1-1)

Pilot performance can be seriously degraded by both prescribed and over-the-counter medications, as well as by the medical conditions for which they are taken. The regulations prohibit pilots from performing crewmember duties while using any medication that affects the faculties in any way contrary to safety. The safest rule is not to fly as a crewmember while taking any medication, unless approved to do so by the FAA.

18. Discuss the effects of nitrogen excesses during scuba diving upon a pilot or passenger in flight. (AIM 8-1-2)

A pilot or passenger who intends to fly after scuba diving should allow the body sufficient time to rid itself of excess nitrogen absorbed during diving. If not, decompression sickness due to evolved gas can occur during exposure to low altitude and create a serious inflight emergency. The recommended waiting times before flight are as follows:

Flight altitudes up to 8,000 feet:

- Wait at least 12 hours after diving which has not required a controlled ascent.
- Wait at least 24 hours after diving which has required controlled ascent.

Flight altitudes above 8,000 feet:

- Wait at least 24 hours after any scuba dive.

Note: The recommended altitudes are actual flight altitudes above mean sea level and not pressurized cabin altitudes. This takes into consideration the risk of decompression of the aircraft during flight.

19. You recently experienced a bad cold and were treated by your personal physician. You continue to take the medications your physician prescribed, but feel much better. Can you resume flying on your current medical or must you first see an FAA Airman Medical Examiner? (14 CFR 61.53)

Anytime you experience an illness or an injury that you feel may affect your ability to safely fly an aircraft, you must self-ground yourself until you feel better. 14 CFR 61.53 requires that all pilots voluntarily self-ground anytime—

Continued

a. They know or have reason to know of any medical condition that would make them unable to meet the requirements for the medical certificate necessary for the pilot operation.

b. They are taking medication or receiving other treatment for a medical condition that results in them being unable to meet the requirements for the medical certificate necessary for the pilot operation.

If in doubt about your condition or the medications you are taking, consult with an AME before resuming your flying activities.

20. Can you operate an aircraft while taking an over-the-counter medication for an on-going condition (allergies, hay fever, etc.)? (FAA-P-8740-41)

Self-medication or taking medication in any form while you are flying can be extremely hazardous. Even simple home or over-the-counter remedies such as aspirin, laxatives, tranquilizers and appetite suppressors may seriously impair the judgment and coordination needed while flying. The safest rule is to take no medicine while flying, except with the advice of your AME.

B. Single-Pilot Resource Management

1. Define the term "single-pilot resource management." (FAA-H-8083-9)

Single-pilot resource management (SRM) is the art and science of managing all the resources (both on-board the aircraft and from outside sources) available to a single pilot (prior to and during flight) to ensure that the successful outcome of the flight is never in doubt. SRM helps pilots learn to execute methods of gathering information, analyzing it, and making decisions.

2. What are examples of the skills necessary for effective SRM? (FAA-H-8083-25)

SRM includes the concepts of aeronautical decision making (ADM), risk management (RM), task management (TM), automation management (AM), controlled flight into terrain (CFIT) awareness, and situational awareness (SA).

3. **What practical application provides a pilot with an effective method to practice SRM?** (FAA-H-8083-9)

   The "Five P" checklist consists of "the Plan, the Plane, the Pilot, the Passengers, and the Programming." It is based on the idea that the pilot has essentially five variables that impact his or her environment and that can cause the pilot to make a single critical decision, or several less critical decisions, that when added together can create a critical outcome.

4. **Explain the use of the "Five P" model to assess risk associated with each of the five factors.** (FAA-H-8083-2)

   At key decision points, application of the Five P checklist should be performed by reviewing each of the critical variables:

   Plan—weather, route, publications, ATC reroutes/delays, fuel onboard/remaining

   Plane—mechanical status, automation status, database currency, backup systems

   Pilot—illness, medication, stress, alcohol, fatigue, eating

   Passengers—pilots/non-pilots, nervous or quiet, experienced or new, business or pleasure

   Programming—autopilot, GPS, MFD/PFD; anticipate likely reroutes/clearances; questions to ask—What is it doing? Why is it doing it? Did I do it?

5. **When is the use of the "Five P" checklist recommended?** (FAA-H-8083-9)

   The "Five P" concept relies on the pilot to adopt a scheduled review of the critical variables at points in the flight where decisions are most likely to be effective. These key decision points include preflight, pre-takeoff, hourly or at the midpoint of the flight, pre-descent, and just prior to the final approach fix (or, for VFR operations, just prior to entering the traffic pattern). They also should be used anytime an emergency situation arises.

C. Aeronautical Decision Making

1. Define the term "aeronautical decision making." (FAA-H-8083-9)

Aeronautical decision making (ADM) is a systematic approach to the mental process used by aircraft pilots to consistently determine the best course of action in response to a given set of circumstances.

2. Explain the basic steps in the decision making process. (FAA-H-8083-9)

a. Define the problem.

b. Choose a course of action.

c. Implement the decision.

d. Evaluate the outcome.

3. What two models are commonly used when practicing aeronautical decision making? (FAA-H-8083-9)

The DECIDE model and the 3P model.

4. The DECIDE model of decision making involves which elements? (FAA-H-8083-2)

D etect a change needing attention.
E stimate the need to counter or react to a change.
C hoose the most desirable outcome for the flight.
I dentify actions to successfully control the change.
D o something to adapt to the change.
E valuate the effect of the action countering the change.

5. How is the 3P model different from the DECIDE model of ADM? (FAA-H-8083-2)

The 3P process is a continuous loop of the pilot's handling of hazards. The DECIDE model and naturalistic decision making focus on particular problems requiring resolution. Therefore, pilots exercise the 3P process continuously, while the DECIDE model and naturalistic decision making result from the 3P process.

6. **Name five hazardous attitudes that can affect a pilot's ability to make sound decisions and properly exercise authority.** (FAA-H-8083-9)

Attitude	Antidote
Anti-authority	Follow the rules—they are usually right.
Impulsivity	Think first—not so fast.
Invulnerability	It could happen to me.
Macho	Taking chances is foolish.
Resignation	I can make a difference, I am not helpless.

7. **What is the first step towards neutralizing a hazardous attitude?** (FAA-H-8083-25)

Recognition of hazardous thoughts is the first step toward neutralizing them. After recognizing a thought as hazardous, the pilot should label it as hazardous, and then state the corresponding antidote. Antidotes should be memorized for each of the hazardous attitudes so they automatically come to mind when needed.

D. Risk Management

1. **Define the term "risk management."** (FAA-H-8083-9)

Risk management is a decision-making process designed to systematically identify hazards, assess the degree of risk, and determine the best course of action. It is a logical process of weighing the potential costs of risks against the possible benefits of allowing those risks to stand uncontrolled.

2. **What is the definition of a "hazard"?** (FAA-H-8083-2)

A hazard is a present condition, event, object, or circumstance that could lead to or contribute to an unplanned or undesired event such as an accident.

3. What are several examples of aviation hazards? (FAA-H-8083-2)

a. A nick in the propeller blade

b. Improper refueling of an aircraft

c. Pilot fatigue

d. Use of unapproved hardware on aircraft

e. Weather

4. What is the definition of "risk"? (FAA-H-8083-2)

Risk is the future impact of a hazard that is not controlled or eliminated.

5. How can the use of the "PAVE" checklist during flight planning help you to assess risk? (FAA-H-8083-9)

Use of the PAVE checklist provides pilots with a simple way to remember each category to examine for risk during flight planning. The pilot divides the risks of flight into four categories:

Pilot-In-Command—general health, physical/mental/emotional state, proficiency, currency

Aircraft—airworthiness, equipment, performance capability

enVironment—weather hazards, terrain, airports/runways to be used, conditions

External pressures—meetings, people waiting at destination, desire to impress someone, etc.

6. Explain the use of a "personal minimums" checklist and how it can help a pilot control risk. (FAA-H-8083-9)

One of the most important concepts that safe pilots understand is the difference between what is "legal" in terms of the regulations, and what is "smart" or "safe" in terms of pilot experience and proficiency. One way a pilot can control the risks is to set personal minimums for items in each risk category. These are limits unique to that individual pilot's current level of experience and proficiency.

7. What is one method you can use to control and manage risk? (FAA-H-8083-2)

One way a pilot can limit exposure to risks is to set personal minimums for items in each risk category, again using PAVE. These are limits unique to that individual pilot's current level of experience and proficiency:

Pilot—experience/recency (takeoffs/landings, hours make/model), physical/mental condition (IMSAFE)

Aircraft—fuel reserves VFR day/night, aircraft performance (W&B, density altitude, etc.), aircraft equipment (avionics familiarity, charts, survival gear)

EnVironment—airport conditions (runway condition/length), weather (winds, ceilings, visibilities)

External pressures—allowance for delays, diversion, cancelation, alternate plans, personal equipment available for alternate plans (phone numbers, credit cards, medications)

8. Explain the use of a personal checklist such as"I'M SAFE" to determine personal risks. (FAA-H-8083-9)

Personal, self-assessment checklists assist pilots in conducting preflight checks on themselves, reviewing their physical and emotional states that could have an effect on their performance. The "I'M SAFE" checklist reminds pilots to consider the following:

Illness—Do I have any symptoms?

Medication—Have I been taking prescription or over-the-counter drugs?

Stress—Am I under psychological pressure from my job? Do I have money, family or health problems?

Alcohol—Have I been drinking within 8 hours? Within 24 hours?

Fatigue—Am I tired and not adequately rested?

Emotions—Am I fully recovered from any extremely upsetting events?

9. Describe how the 3P model can be used for practical risk management. (FAA-H-8083-2)

The Perceive, Process, Perform (3P) model for risk management offers a simple, practical, and systematic approach that can be used during all phases of flight. To use it, pilots will:

Perceive—the hazards for a flight, which are present events, objects, or circumstances that could contribute to an undesired future event, given set of circumstances for a flight; think through circumstances related to the PAVE risk categories. The fundamental question to ask is, "what could hurt me, my passengers, or my aircraft?"

Process—the hazards by evaluating their impact on flight safety. Think through the Consequences of each hazard, Alternatives available, Reality of the situation, and External pressures (CARE) that might influence their analysis.

Perform—by implementing the best course of action. Transfer (can the risk decision be transferred to someone else? can you consult someone?); Eliminate (is there a way to eliminate the hazard?); Accept (do the benefits of accepting risk outweigh the costs?); Mitigate (what can you do to reduce the risk?) (TEAM)

10. Explain how often a pilot should use the 3P model of ADM throughout a flight. (FAA-H-8083-9)

Once a pilot has completed the 3P decision process and selected a course of action, the process begins again because the circumstances brought about by the course of action require analysis. The decision-making process is a continuous loop of perceiving, processing and performing.

E. Task Management

1. Define the term "task management." (FAA-H-8083-9)

Task management is the process by which pilots manage the many, concurrent tasks that must be performed to safely and efficiently operate an aircraft.

2. What are several factors that can reduce a pilot's ability to manage workload effectively? (FAA-H-8083-25)

Environmental conditions—temperature and humidity extremes, noise, vibration, and lack of oxygen.

Physiological stress—fatigue, lack of physical fitness, sleep loss, missed meals (leading to low blood sugar levels), and illness.

Psychological stress—social or emotional factors, such as a death in the family, a divorce, a sick child, or a demotion at work. This type of stress may also be related to mental workload, such as analyzing a problem, navigating an aircraft, or making decisions.

3. What are several options that a pilot can employ to decrease workload and avoid becoming overloaded? (FAA-H-8083-25)

Stop, think, slow down, and prioritize. Tasks such as locating an item on a chart or setting a radio frequency may be delegated to another pilot or passenger; an autopilot, if available, may be used; or ATC may be enlisted to provide assistance.

4. What is one method of prioritizing tasks to avoid an overload situation? (FAA-H-8083-25)

During any situation, and especially in an emergency, remember the phrase "aviate, navigate, and communicate."

5. How can tasks be completed in a timely manner without causing a distraction from flying? (FAA-H-8083-9)

By planning, prioritizing, and sequencing tasks, a potential work overload situation can be avoided. As experience is gained, a pilot learns to recognize future workload requirements and can prepare for high workload periods during times of low workload.

6. Why are pilots encouraged to use checklists? (FAA-H-8083-3)

The checklist is an aid to the memory and helps to ensure that critical items necessary for the safe operation of aircraft are not overlooked or forgotten. They provide a standardized method for verifying aircraft configuration and a logical sequence for accomplishing tasks inside and outside the cockpit.

7. **What are two common methods of checklist usage?** (Order 8900.1)

   a. *Do-Verify (DV) method*—consists of the checklist being accomplished in a variable sequence without a preliminary challenge. After all of the action items on the checklist have been completed, the checklist is then read again while each item is verified. The DV method allows the pilot/flightcrew to use flow patterns from memory to accomplish a series of actions quickly and efficiently.

   b. *Challenge-Do-Verify (CDV) method*—consists of a pilot/ crewmember making a challenge before an action is initiated, taking the action, and then verifying that the action item has been accomplished. The CDV method is most effective in two-pilot crews where one crewmember issues the challenge and the second crewmember takes the action and responds to the first crewmember, verifying that the action was taken.

8. **What are several examples of common errors that can occur when using a checklist?** (FAA-H-8083-3)

   a. Checklist items are missed because of distraction or interruption (by passengers, ATC, etc.).

   b. Checklist items are incorrectly performed (hurrying checklist; reading item but not verifying or setting).

   c. Failure to use the appropriate checklist for a specific phase of flight.

   d. Too much time spent with head down, reading the checklist and compromising safety.

   e. Checklist is not readily accessible in cockpit.

   f. Emergency/abnormal procedures checklist is not readily available.

   g. Memory items accomplished but not confirmed with checklist.

9. **In what phases of flight should a prepared checklist be used?** (FAA-H-8083-3)

   a. Preflight inspection

   b. Before engine start

   c. Engine starting

   d. Before taxiing

e. Before takeoff

f. After takeoff

g. Cruise

h. Descent

i. Before landing

j. After landing

k. Engine shutdown and securing

10. What are several recommended methods for managing checklist accomplishment? (Order 8900.1)

a. The pilot should touch/point at each control, display or switch.

b. Verbally state the desired status of the checklist item.

c. When complete, announce that "___ checklist is complete."

11. What are "immediate action" items? (Order 8900.1)

An immediate action item is an action that must be accomplished so expeditiously (in order to avoid or stabilize a hazardous situation) that time is not available for the pilot/crewmember to refer to a manual or checklist. Once the emergency has been brought under control, the pilot refers to the actual checklist to verify that all action items were accomplished. Only after this is done should the remainder of the checklist be completed.

F. Situational Awareness

1. Define the term "situational awareness." (FAA-H-8083-25)

Situational awareness (SA) is the accurate perception and understanding of all the factors and conditions within the five fundamental risk elements (flight, pilot, aircraft, environment, external pressures) that affect safety before, during, and after the flight.

2. **What are some of the elements inside and outside the aircraft that a pilot must consider to maintain situational awareness?** (FAA-H-8083-9)

   Inside the aircraft—the status of aircraft systems, pilot, and passengers

   Outside the aircraft—awareness of where the aircraft is in relation to terrain, traffic, weather, and airspace

3. **What are several factors that reduce situational awareness?** (FAA-H-8083-15)

   Factors that reduce SA include fatigue, distractions, unusual or unexpected events, complacency, high workload, unfamiliar situations, and inoperative equipment.

4. **When flying a technically advanced aircraft (TAA), what are several procedures that help ensure that situational awareness is enhanced, not diminished, by the automation?** (FAA-H-8083-25)

   Two basic procedures are to always double-check the system and to use verbal callouts. At a minimum, ensure the presentation makes sense. Was the correct destination fed into the navigation system? Callouts, even for single-pilot operations, are an excellent way to maintain situational awareness as well as manage information.

5. **What additional procedures can be used for maintaining situational awareness in technically advanced aircraft?** (FAA-H-8083-25)

   a. Perform verification checks of all programming prior to departure.

   b. Check the flight routing—ensure all routing matches the planned route of flight.

   c. Always verify waypoints.

   d. Make use of all onboard navigation equipment—use VOR to backup GPS, and vice versa.

   e. Match the use of the automated system with pilot proficiency— stay within personal limitations.

f. Plan a realistic flight route to maintain situational awareness—ATC doesn't always give you direct routing.

g. Be ready to verify computer data entries—incorrect keystrokes can lead to loss of situational awareness.

G. CFIT Awareness

1. A majority of controlled flight into terrain (CFIT) accidents have been attributed to what factors? (AC 61-134)

a. Lack of pilot currency

b. Loss of situational awareness

c. Pilot distractions and breakdown of SRM

d. Failure to comply with minimum safe altitudes

e. Breakdown in effective ADM

f. Insufficient planning, especially for the descent and arrival segments

2. A pilot can decrease the likelihood of a CFIT accident at the destination by identifying what risk factors prior to flight? (AC 61-134)

Factors such as airport location, runway lighting, weather/daylight conditions, approach specifications, ATC capabilities and limitations, type of operation, departure procedures, controller/pilot phraseology, and crew configuration should all be considered prior to flight.

3. Describe several operational techniques that will help you avoid a CFIT accident. (AC 61-134)

a. Maintain situational awareness at all times.

b. Adhere to safe takeoff and departure procedures.

c. Familiarize yourself with surrounding terrain features and obstacles.

d. Adhere to published routes and minimum altitudes.

Continued

e. Fly a stabilized approach.

f. Understand ATC clearances and instructions.

g. Don't become complacent.

H. Automation Management

1. What does the term "automation management" refer to? (FAA-H-8083-9)

Automation management is the demonstrated ability to control and navigate an aircraft by means of the automated systems installed in the aircraft.

2. In what three areas must a pilot be proficient when using advanced avionics or any automated system? (FAA-H-8083-25)

The pilot must know what to expect, how to monitor the system for proper operation, and be prepared to promptly take appropriate action if the system does not perform as expected.

3. What is the most important aspect of managing an autopilot/FMS? (FAA-H-8083-9)

Knowing at all times which modes are engaged, which modes are armed to engage, and being capable of verifying that armed functions (e.g. navigation tracking or altitude capture) engage at the appropriate time.

4. At a minimum, the pilot flying with advanced avionics must know how to manage what three primary items? (FAA-H-8083-25)

The course deviation indicator (CDI), the navigation source, and the autopilot.

5. **Automation management is a good place to practice the standard callout technique. What are standard callouts?** (FAA-H-8083-16)

To assist in maintaining situational awareness, professional flight crews often use standard callouts. For example, the non-flying pilot may call 2,000 and 1,000 feet prior to reaching an assigned altitude. The callout may be, "two to go" and "one to go." Single pilot operations can also benefit from this practice by adopting standard set callouts that can be used in the different segments of a flight. Examples of standard callouts are: "Power Set", "Airspeed Alive", "Rotate", "Positive Rate—Gear Up", "Localizer Alive", "Glideslope Alive", "Nav Source Verified", "Approach Mode Armed", "Approach Mode Active", "Final Approach Fix", etc.

Additional Study Questions

1. What are several factors that may contribute to a pilot's impaired performance? (AIM 8-1-1)

2. Define spatial disorientation, and give several examples of illusions that can lead to it. (AIM 8-1-5)

3. Optical or visual illusions can increase the risk of an incident or accident occurring, even to the most experienced pilots. What can pilots do to mitigate that risk? (FAA-H-8083-2)

4. When should a pilot be particularly alert for the possibility of carbon monoxide poisoning? (AIM 8-1-4)

5. What is sinus block and what are the symptoms? How can it be prevented? (AIM 8-1-2)

6. Most pilots are goal-oriented, which can sometimes result in a tendency to ignore established personal limitations in favor of completing a flight. How can a pilot mitigate the risk involved when this occurs? (FAA-H-8083-2)

7. When planning a cross-country flight, how can a pilot mitigate the risk of inadvertent VFR into IMC? (FAA-H-8083-25)

8. You have the proper charts, you planned your route of flight, and have a detailed navigation log. Once airborne, you decide that it's much easier to let the automation fly the airplane and manage the navigation. You will handle the communications and monitor the automation. Explain what the hazards are in this scenario. (FAA-H-8083-2)

9. How can a pilot mitigate the risk of the potentially dangerous distractions that can occur when flying with advanced avionics? (FAA-H-8083-2)

Scenario-Based Training

by Arlynn McMahon

9

Introduction

Pilot examiners are encouraged by the FAA to develop a scenario as part of the "Plan of Action" used during the practical tests they conduct. Usually, the examiner will ask the applicant to pre-plan a cross-country. The assigned cross-country, then, is the beginning of the scenario and is the basis for this part of the oral exam.

The examiner is not required to follow the order of Tasks as they appear in the Airman Certification Standards (ACS). Therefore the questions in this chapter are presented as they might appear in an actual oral exam, rather than in the order given in the ACS. However, these questions alone do not make a complete oral exam. Usually, the examiner will first ask a scenario-based question, and then building from your response, construct additional questions as he or she goes in order to further probe into your knowledge of a ACS Task.

Scenario-questions are intentionally open-ended. Don't get frustrated. They are designed to allow you to go freely in any direction that you feel is pertinent in demonstrating your ability to apply aeronautical knowledge and to be a safe pilot.

Answers to scenario-questions can be lengthy. Feel free to use scrap paper to organize your thoughts before answering. For example, "TOMATO FLAMES" by itself is not a suitable answer to a question, but writing this acronym on a piece of paper will help you organize a better answer as you begin reciting the required equipment. Draw a diagram if that helps you to discuss the fuel system or to more clearly describe a concept to the examiner.

Ideally, your responses to scenario-questions will demonstrate that you understand the underlying concepts of what's important and why. This is the *Practical Test*. To perform your best, you need to convey the practical application of *what* to do, *when* to do it, *why* do it, or *how* to do it.

Aeronautical decision making (ADM) is a "special emphasis area" on the Practical Test. Feel free to "think out loud" so the examiner can hear the reasoning in your answers. Discuss the plans you considered but discarded, and why you did so. By all means, include the elements that you feel make a "good" pilot, rather than one who just meets minimum standards. Show that you are prepared to be a responsible aviation-citizen.

The questions in this scenario-based training chapter are worded similarly to the way that the designated examiner might ask them during your exam, and your answers should reflect the specifics of the scenario presented to you. Scenario-questions don't have one universal correct answer; your correct answers will depend on the presented scenario, the specific aircraft used for the practical exam and preparations you completed in planning the cross-country.

For this reason, the answers provided here indicate the concepts your answer should or could include, but for your exam you should revise them with your specific information as necessary. Also included with many of the answers are tips, suggestions or notes (in *italic* type), which draw attention to the specific areas you should address in your responses to the examiner's questions.

Scenario-Based Questions

1. **Your good friend has requested you to fly as safety pilot in his retractable gear Piper Arrow while he practices flight by reference to instruments. What do regulations require for you to be able to do this?**

   Your answer should include knowledge of safety pilot requirements, currency requirements to carry passengers, and the requirements for a complex endorsement.

   I must meet safety pilot requirements, currency requirements to carry passengers, and the requirements for a complex endorsement, including:

   • To be a safety pilot I must hold at least a private pilot certificate with single-engine land.

   • I must be endorsed to act as PIC in a complex airplane.

   • I must hold a valid medical certificate.

   • I must have satisfactorily met the requirements of a flight review, and

   • I must have logged at least 3 takeoffs and landings in the preceding 90 days to carry passengers.

2. **What personal items will you take with you to ensure that you are legal for this flight, carrying me as your passenger?**

   • Pilot certificate, photo ID and a current medical certificate (duration based on age). These must be available in the cockpit.

- Verify in the logbook the following were completed:
  - › A flight review (or equivalency) within the previous 24 months.
  - › 3 takeoffs and landings within the previous 90 days (to a full stop if at night).

3. Tell me about the FAA Pilot Proficiency Program (WINGS).

A good pilot is always in training, even after passing the practical exam. The FAA Pilot Proficiency Program:

- is an FAA and industry accident prevention initiative.
- is based on the premise that pilots who maintain proficiency are safer pilots.
- encourages on-going flight training and aviation education.
- is accomplished in little bits, throughout the year, encouraging pilots to fly in different seasons and in different flight conditions.
- satisfies the flight review recency requirement as prescribed in 61.56(e), as long as the requirements for at least the "basic WINGS" level are met within the preceding 24 months.
- has its official home at www.faasafety.gov, where free on-line courses are available.
- specifics of the program are outlined in Advisory Circular 61-91.

4. Let's talk about the plane: How do you know that it is "airworthy"?

An airplane's airworthiness involves 3 different levels of verification:

- The Airworthiness Certificate proves that the aircraft was manu-factured in compliance with Regulations.
- The maintenance technician having an Inspector Authorization (IA certificate) certifies the airworthiness at least annually by the "return to service" statement upon completion of the annual inspection.
- The pilot certifies airworthiness, and is the final authority, before each flight with a thorough preflight inspection and inspection status review.

5. Prove to me the airplane is airworthy for our flight today.

Include required inspections, documents, and instruments/equipment, as well as your statement that the preflight inspection shows the aircraft to be satisfactory.

Here are my pertinent aircraft documents and papers:

- Airworthiness Certificate.
- Registration.
- Operating Limitations *[which is probably in the AFM or POH]*— and here are the placards and markings on the instruments *[when appropriate]*.
- Weight and Balance Data.

Regarding the aircraft maintenance records for this airplane:

- The annual inspection was completed within the past 12 months and a repairman with an Inspector Authorization stated that the aircraft was "Returned To Service."
- The 100-hour inspection was completed *[if appropriate]*.
- The transponder inspection was completed within the previous 24 months *[if appropriate]*.
- The ELT battery is current and the system was inspected within the previous 12 months.
- Airworthiness Directives are complied with.
- Outstanding maintenance discrepancies have been checked and the status of inoperative equipment verified.

Also, the aircraft has the required instruments and equipment (i.e., day VFR versus night VFR); a thorough preflight inspection has been completed, the aircraft is properly serviced and it is in airworthy condition—safe for this flight.

6. You planned a cross-country. Show me your true course, and what items you considered when choosing this course.

For extra credit and to demonstrate good ADM, experienced instructors suggest you discuss alternative courses that were considered but discarded, and why.

My chosen course considered:

- Terrain—and I considered circumnavigating extreme high terrain, or areas of dense forest with no possible emergency landing areas.
- Checkpoints that are easy to see and identify.
- Navigation and communication reception—I considered altering course and/or altitude for reliable reception.
- Airspace—I considered altering course and/or altitude to avoid SUA and Class B airspace, etc.
- Weather avoidance.

7. Immediately after takeoff, you're at 100 feet AGL when your kneeboard falls onto the floor. You reach down to get it and suddenly become aware of a buffeting feeling. What should you be concerned about?

Demonstrate here that you recognize and understand stalls and spins, and know how to recover from them.

My first concern is to immediately get the nose down—reduce the angle of attack.

- The buffeting means the aircraft is on the brink of an unintended stall without having sufficient altitude to recover.
- The distraction may also mean that the aircraft is not in coordinated flight.

8. **Beginning with takeoff, and along your true course until landing, talk me through the different airspace we will fly through, and what implications each has on our flight.**

Use the sectional chart and begin with the airspace surrounding your departure airport, then proceed along your route, describing each airspace area as you come to it and how it may impact your flight. Continue describing the airspace and special use airspace as you encounter it along your route, and mention how that airspace may impact your decisions and requirements to be there—or not be there!

- Class D airspace extends to the blue dashed line—while in this area I must maintain two-way communications with the control tower.
- Assuming a normal climb, by the time I clear the "D" airspace, I'll be above 700 feet AGL. At this point, I will be at the area depicted on the chart where the base of the Class E airspace is at 700 feet AGL. Therefore, I am required to maintain VFR cloud clearances and 3 SM visibility.
  › If I'm not above 700 feet AGL, then I'll be in Class G airspace where I'm required to remain clear of the clouds and at least 1 SM visibility.
- Further along the course, I'm now in an area where the base of Class E airspace is at 1,200 AGL.

9. **Why did you choose this altitude?**

Consider the following, as appropriate for your planned flight:
- Terrain clearances—high enough to exceed minimum safe altitudes. As a new pilot, I will fly at least 1,500 feet AGL.
- Cloud clearances—it meets the requirements (for example, 500 feet below the clouds).
- Direction of flight—complies with regulations.
- Airspace—stays clear of any airspace I'd rather not fly close to or into (such as TFRs, prohibited, or restricted areas).
- Favorable winds—a suitable altitude that allows the most favorable ground speed.
- Allows me to see visual checkpoints easily.
- Best for aircraft performance (true airspeed vs. economic fuel burn).
- Personal minimums—this is an altitude I feel comfortable flying and allows safety margins.

10. Looking at your Nav Log, how did you calculate fuel requirements?

Here, demonstrate your ability to use performance charts and graphs located in the POH/AFM. Calculate precisely, but add a safety margin at the end; also, remember to apply any and all pertinent notes included in the performance charts. Show and discuss your precise calculations (do not round-off, do not add "fudge factors").

Here are my precise calculations for:

- Fuel required for start, runup and taxi.
- Fuel for takeoff and climb.
- The chosen power setting and its associated fuel flow for the duration of cruise.
- Fuel required for descent and landing.
- +30 minutes for required fuel reserve.

In addition to the above, I added fuel as necessary to meet my personal safety minimums (for example, a new pilot should carry enough fuel to fly to a suitable alternate airport or +30 minutes cruise fuel after that—a total 1 hour reserve).

11. You are required to prepare a navigation log. Why is having a nav log important?

Demonstrate your own routine use of a nav log.

I use a nav log because:

- "All available information" is organized on one piece of paper—that's good cockpit management.
- It provides a mental rehearsal and preparation for each aspect of the flight—that's good situational awareness.
- During flight, it is used to monitor the plan by:
  - › Verifying ground speeds and fuel consumption.
  - › Verifying ETAs to checkpoints and final destination.
  - › Helping me in thinking and planning ahead.
  - › Helping to prevent me from getting lost.
  - › Reminding me of routine cockpit tasks (change fuel tanks, listen to ATIS, cancel flight plan, etc.).
  - › Assisting in diversion to an alternate, if it should become necessary.

12. **When planning a cross-country that will require a fuel stop, what factors do you feel are important in selecting an airport for a stop?**

Demonstrate here your understanding of aeronautical decision making.

In selecting an airport for a fuel stop, important factors to consider include:

- Airport airspace—airspace similar to my training and/or experience.
- Runways—length and relation to the wind.
- Size of the airport—not too small but not so big that the amount and type of traffic is intimidating.
- Pilot support facilities available (FSS access, weather station, hours of operation, etc.)
- Amenities (restrooms, service, loaner car, restaurant on the airport, etc.)
- Price of fuel or method for payment.

13. **Considering your calculated takeoff distance for our flight, how would that change if the outside air temperature were 20° warmer or 20° cooler?**

Your specific answer to this question will depend on the individual circumstances of your practical exam; but whatever your situation is, the answer should demonstrate your ability to accurately use the performance table and your understanding of the effects of atmospheric conditions on the airplane's performance. You should include the table or chart in your aircraft's POH, specifically:

- *How your calculations were carefully performed. Interpolate as necessary for accuracy and apply any "Notes" that may be applicable.*
- *Re-calculate performance using the 20° warmer and 20° cooler scenarios.*

Discuss the differences in performance and effects of density altitude on performance, not only for takeoff but through each of the phases of flight.

14. Are the runways you plan to use today suitable for us?

Demonstrate your ability to use the performance tables in your aircraft's POH and your understanding for the need to include a safety margin. Show your calculations.

Yes, using the takeoff and landing performance charts, I calculated the required distance to takeoff and to land. This shows what the aircraft is capable of; however, as a new pilot, I am not always able to achieve takeoffs or landings that precisely—so, I added 50% *[or whatever your safety margin is]* more to my calculations as my personal minimum when determining runway suitability.

15. During our flight today, with whom will you communicate?

Demonstrate your knowledge of available resources and your willingness to use them.

- Ground/Tower/Departure (if departing from a controlled airport), or
- Unicom or Multicom (if from an uncontrolled airport).
- Enroute: Flight Following to assist in knowing about pop-up TFRs and to assist with traffic avoidance.
- FSS for update weather, altimeter settings and possible revisions to the filed flight plan.
- Destination airport communications *[as appropriate to the destination]*.

16. How did you obtain weather information for our flight?

- Beginning last night, I watched the weather channel on TV. The weather channel is not a specific aviation weather source, but it helps me to hear the meteorologist talk about the weather patterns.
- Then I logged online to DUATS and received an outlook briefing.
- This morning I logged on to DUATS for a standard weather briefing to complete my planning and nav log.
- I was confused about an abbreviation that I didn't know, so I called Flight Service and got their help.
- Then about 1 hour ago I called FSS again for an abbreviated weather briefing, just to make sure that nothing had changed since this morning's briefing.

17. Tell me about the weather along our flight.

Demonstrate your understanding of meteorology and what entails a complete weather briefing.

My standard weather briefing shows:
- Pressure areas affecting weather.
- Fronts affecting weather and their direction of movement.
- Ceilings, winds and visibility at departure, at several points en route and at the destination.
- Wind direction and speed at cruise altitude.
- Significant or adverse weather near the route or during possible flight time, and how it may affect the flight; it includes a plan to escape a possible problem of this kind.
- NOTAMs.

18. Tell me about 2 different weather charts that you used in preparing for our flight and how you used them.

It's easy to get confused when discussing these charts. To make answering this question easier, bring print-outs to the exam of the charts you used and show them as you answer.

- I used the **surface analysis chart** to see the pressure areas, fronts, wind, local weather, and visual obstructions. It is transmitted every 3 hours and covers the country.
- I used the **weather depiction chart** to get an overview of the surface conditions as derived from METAR and other surface observations. It gives me an overall picture of the weather across the United States. It is transmitted every 3 hours.
- I used the **significant weather prognostic chart** to see the forecast. The chart has four-panels that include 12- and 24-hour forecasts. Charts are issued four times a day. The valid time is printed on each panel. The upper two panels show forecast significant weather, which may include turbulence, freezing levels, and IFR or MVFR weather.

19. Tell me about 2 different weather forecasts that you used in preparing for our flight and how you used them.

Include, as appropriate for your flight planning purposes, details of weather forecasts such as:

- I used the **area forecast** to get the big picture about the general weather in the area, what is causing the weather, and how it may change during the upcoming 24 hours.

- I used the **TAF** to get specific weather for certain weather reporting areas along my route, and for how conditions at those airports may change. This allows me to evaluate if the clouds and visibility will allow my flight to continue VFR. I could also find areas of VFR in case I run into unforecasted weather that I need to escape.

- I used the **winds and temperatures aloft forecast**. With the wind direction and velocity, I found the most desirable altitude giving the best ground speeds. I also used the temperatures aloft to determine probable altitudes for clouds to form.

20. How will you obtain updated weather information while enroute?

Demonstrate your understanding of all resources available and how to choose the best resource to use in a given situation. For example:

- I will use technology. (As an example, the GNS530 or G1000 supplies weather information. Handheld units such as the GNS 396, 496 or 696 supply weather, etc.). But technology by itself shouldn't be used to make decisions—there are too many problems with updating and interpreting the information.

- If I only need recorded information (for instance, to update an altimeter setting), I could listen to a nearby AWOS/ASOS/ATIS. Also, the HIWAS has valuable updated weather information in a recorded format.

- If I need to ask questions (for example, if I guess that weather is unexpectedly changing), I would contact FSS on 122.4 or one of the remote transmitters associated with a VOR.

- If I'm in a pinch, or if the flight is becoming unsafe, ATC might be of assistance.

- For the best weather update, I would collect information from a variety of resources before making a decision.

21. While enroute, we listen to the ATIS of a Class D airport near our course to update the altimeter setting and find that the ATIS is reporting visibility as 2 SM. What does that mean for us?

Demonstrate your understating of VFR weather minimums in Class E and Class G airspace, and the special VFR clearance. Show your aeronautical decision making ability by evaluating your options and choosing the best option based on the specifics of your flight.

We have 2 priorities: (1) to remain legal, and (2) as a new pilot, the prudent choice is an immediate diversion to an alternate airport to land.

• Option 1 is to fly in "G" airspace, where regulations allow us to remain clear of clouds with 1 SM visibility while enroute to an uncontrolled airport and land.

• Option 2 is to fly in "G" airspace while heading for the Class D airport and request a special VFR from ATC to land there.

22. You have chosen to divert to an airport that you were not intending to visit. How will you obtain the needed information about your alternate airport?

Demonstrate your understanding of all resources available and how to choose the best resource for a given situation. For extra credit, mention that you would turn on the autopilot to help relieve workload while researching information.

The most pressing information needed is airport airspace, runway length, airport elevation, and an airport communication frequency. I would:

• use technology—most GPS databases include all of this information.

• use the sectional chart—the needed information is on the airport legend.

• use the *Chart Supplement U.S.*

• use a combination of the above.

23. What deice or anti-ice equipment is your airplane equipped with?

Demonstrate that you know the specific equipment installed on your airplane, as well as when to use it.

- Defrost—used to keep the windshield clear. Turn it on in advance of a possible icing situation.
- Pitot heat—used to keep the pitot/static instruments operational. Turn it on in advance of a possible icing situation.
- Carburetor heat—used to keep fuel and air flowing to the engine. It's normally turned on after the first sign of possible carburetor icing.
- The most important piece of equipment is a thinking pilot who, when encountering dangerous icing conditions, can make a timely decision to turn around or land as soon as practical.

24. Tell me about the fuel system on your airplane.

Include the components of your airplane's fuel system, the normal operation of the system, and how you interact with it. Be specific, using the information contained in the POH for your airplane. The following answer, based on an example airplane, illustrates the type of details you might cover.

- Twenty-eight gallons are stored in each wing tank. Three gallons are unusable and a total of 53 gallons are usable. I would order and verify that 100LL is being serviced into the airplane.
- Fuel quantity is measured by float-type quantity indicators, but good pilots always verify the fuel visually. Annunciators show L and R "LOW FUEL" if the fuel quantity is below 5 gallons in a tank.
- The tank has a visual FUEL TAB, allowing verification that 17.5 gallons are on board when takeoffs are performed with less than full fuel.
- The tanks are vented and I ensure the vents are not blocked during the preflight inspection.
- Also on the preflight inspection, I drain fuel from 13 fuel sumps to verify fuel grade and to remove any possible sediment. Ten of these sumps are on the wings, 2 are on the belly, and there is a fuel strainer in the cowling that is pulled to collect a fuel sample.

Continued

- Fuel flows by gravity from the wing tanks to the fuel selector value. I control fuel to the engine being fed from the L, R or BOTH tanks. I select "BOTH" for takeoff, climbs, landings, and maneuvers that involve slips or skids of more than 30 seconds.

- From the fuel selector, fuel flows to a reservoir tank, aux fuel pump, fuel shutoff valve, and into the engine.

- I activate the auxiliary fuel pump for start and during engine emergencies.

- The fuel shutoff valve shuts off fuel to the engine. I activate this to decrease the likelihood of fire upon ditching, and during an extended period of aircraft storage.

25. What method of navigation will you use today and what are the advantages and limitations of that method?

Demonstrate your understanding of navigation methods and resources available and how to choose the best resource to use in a given situation. For extra credit and to demonstrate ADM, point out that the best way to navigate is by using a combination of methods.

Dead Reckoning — Advantages are that it is simple. When everything else fails, it will bring us home. The limitations are that it requires accurate winds and performance calculations, and careful time-keeping.

Pilotage — Advantages: It builds confidence; you see it on the chart and see it on the ground. Limitations: It requires prominent checkpoints and enough visibility to see them.

VOR — Advantages: It's more reliable than dead reckoning or pilotage; an accurate form of navigation over an area where no prominent checkpoints exist. Limitations: Line-of-sight navigation, somewhat dependent on altitude, less accurate when far away from the station.

GPS — Advantages: It is not limited to line-of-sight; ground speed and other calculations are provided. Distance is not slant distance. Limitations: There are occasional outages, and the database must be current for reliable data. Ground speeds are instantaneous but not point-to-point, as is needed for calculating accurate ETAs and fuel remaining.

26. Let's talk about your passenger safety briefing. Assume that I am your good friend who has never been in a small plane. Give me your passenger safety briefing.

The items below (indicated as bold initials of the word "safety") are what you are required to include in a safety briefing. Demonstrate your knowledge of the elements of a complete safety briefing and your understanding that an effective briefing at the start of the flight can add to the safety and enjoyment of the flight for everyone.

S   Seat belts—fastened for taxi, takeoff and landing.
    Shoulder harness—fastened for takeoff and landing.
    Seat—adjusted and locked into place.

A   Air vents—location and operation; you can adjust.
    All environment controls—what's available; you shouldn't adjust (ask me).
    Action in case of passenger discomfort.

F   Fire extinguisher—location and operation.

E   Exit doors (and windows)—how to secure, how to operate.
    Emergency evacuation plan.
    Emergency equipment—location and operation.

T   Traffic (scanning, spotting, and notifying pilot).
    Talking (sterile cockpit expectations).

Y   Your questions? There are no dumb questions. It's more fun when you ask.

27. Enroute you notice a discharge on the ammeter. What will you do?

Demonstrate your understanding of the electrical system, using specifics relevant to your airplane.

A discharge on the ammeter indicates the possibility of an electrical problem. If left unchecked, it might exhaust the battery, causing a partial or total loss of electrical equipment. I would:

- Turn off the avionics master switch (if appropriate) and the master switch to reset what may be an over-voltage relay.
- Turn the master back on and notice the indication on the ammeter. If it is still not showing a charge, then:
  - › Turn off any unnecessary electrical equipment, and
  - › Re-evaluate how this may affect the safety of continued flight.
  - › Consider landing as soon as practical during the day or as soon as possible at night, for repairs.

28. **As you approach the airport of intended landing with your battery now dead, are we in danger of the engine quitting? If not, what problems might we encounter while landing with a dead battery?**

Demonstrate your understanding of the electrical system, using specifics relevant to your airplane.

- No, the engine will not quit; it derives its electrical ignition power from magnetos — not the electrical system.
- We may have to land without flaps — a slip might be needed to descend.
- We will not have engine gauges — the fuel gauges will show empty which is always uncomfortable to see.
- We will not have lights — if at night, a flashlight will be needed in the cockpit. The landing will be made without a landing light.
- We will not have a turn coordinator, but the pitot/static and gyro instruments will be operational.
- We will not have COM radios — if landing at a controlled airport, we should look for light gun signals. If landing at an uncontrolled airport at night, we might not be able to turn on the pilot-controlled lighting.

29. **Are there specific techniques that you normally use for collision avoidance?**

Demonstrate the need for good collision avoidance habits during each phase of flight.

- Ensure that the windshield is as clean as possible.
- Organize the cockpit to avoid a lot of "head down" time — pre-fold charts, pre-select frequencies, etc.
- Keep my head up and eyes outside during all ground maneuvering. On the ground, stop while copying ATC clearances.
- Perform clearing turns before performance maneuvers requiring rapid changes in heading or altitude.
- Scan for traffic often when in straight-and-level flight and during maneuvers.
- Don't practice maneuvers over VORs, airports, or other areas where traffic normally converges.

- Enter traffic patterns correctly and at proper traffic pattern altitude.
- Listen on frequencies, especially at uncontrolled airports, to hear possible traffic in the area.
- Visually verify that final approach is clear before taking the runway for takeoff.
- Use anti-collision lights and a landing light at night and during times of low visibility.
- Comply with right of way rules (14 CFR §91.113).
- In the radar environment, if ATC issues traffic, I look to see it and maneuver to avoid it. If I lose sight of the traffic, I report that to ATC.
- Use flight following en route as another tool for traffic avoidance.

30. **With our head in the cockpit reading the taxi diagram, we accidentally hit a large taxiway light. The prop is chewed up pretty bad and the lower nose cowling is banged up but nothing else seems to be damaged. Are you required to report this to the NTSB?**

This does not require a report to the NTSB because the damage is limited to the prop and the damage to other people's property probably doesn't exceed $25,000. Therefore, I would:

- Have the airplane towed to the maintenance shop for repairs.
- Contact the airport manager to have possible foreign object debris cleaned from the taxiway.

31. Tell me about the emergency equipment and survival gear that is onboard for our flight today.

Show your awareness that the need for emergency equipment and survival gear is not limited to flights over extreme terrain or extreme temperature changes.

If the emergency originates in flight and there is time:

- The autopilot could be considered emergency equipment to help relieve workload.
- The communications radio can be used to send a "mayday."
- The GPS could be used for "NRST" and "DIRECT TO" navigation to an airport.
- The transponder could be used to signal "7700."

I have the following items onboard that could be useful after ditching:

- Fire extinguisher—It is charged and I know how to use it.
- Cell phone
- Water and snacks
- Pocket knife/all-purpose tool
- First aid kit
- Emergency locator transmitter (ELT)—I can manually activate it.
- Other items that I routinely carry that would be of use in an emergency are _____ [if relevant].

32. What do you feel are the major differences between the PAVE checklist and the 5P checklist?

Show your awareness of the need to manage the risks of flight and the tools available to help pilots.

- Both checklists are tools recommended for pilots in managing the risks associated in flying.
- Both consider the risk elements, those are: the pilot, the airplane, the environment and the external factors.
- The PAVE checklist encourages the pilot to react to a risk element that he finds unacceptable.
- The 5P checklist encourages the pilot to be proactive: to do surveillance, look ahead for changes in a risk element, and take early action to prevent a problem.

33. For a flight involving first time fliers as passengers, how would you manage the risks pertaining to their aeromedical factors?

Demonstrate your knowledge of aeromedical factors as well as your understanding of what causes them and how to address them.

- If possible, I would sit the passenger most likely to experience motion sickness in the front seat so I can keep his attention outside—far, far away on the horizon.
- I keep a Sic-Sac onboard in case of motion sickness or hyperventilation.
- If possible, I would sit the passenger most likely to experience ear or sinus problems in the front seat so I can watch for early signs of problems and possibly take corrective action, especially during climbs and descents.

34. Your friend owns a condo in Colorado ski country. It's a long trip from the East Coast. How would you manage the risks pertaining to the aeromedical factors?

Demonstrate your knowledge of relevant aeromedical factors as well as your understanding of what causes them and how to address them.

- I would consider each element of the "I'M SAFE" checklist before takeoff.
- Although the regulations require supplemental oxygen when flying over 12,500 feet for more than 30 minutes, if flying at an altitude of more than 10,000 feet MSL, I would carry supplemental oxygen, especially at night to aid my eyesight.
- Unless terrain (as an example) requires otherwise, I would plan to fly below 8,000 feet MSL to prevent possible hypoxia.
- I would carry a small bottle of water to ward off the possibility of dehydration (but not a big bottle because that might create another problem!).
- Rather than planning long legs (more than 4 hours), I'd plan shorter legs with a fuel/rest stop every 2 to 3 hours to prevent stress and fatigue.

35. You are considering the flight home after a scuba diving vacation during the week of Christmas. You want to enjoy every minute possible in the water and partying on the beach. How would you manage the risks pertaining to aeromedical factors on the flight home?

Demonstrate your knowledge of the relevant aeromedical factors as well as your understanding of what causes them and how to address them.

• I would consider each element of the "I'M SAFE" checklist before takeoff.

• Because it's Christmas week (winter), the cabin heat will be probably be on. I would place the carbon monoxide detector near the heat outlet on the floor of the cabin for the earliest possible detection of carbon monoxide.

• Winter may involve snow showers. If flying in low visibility conditions, I scan instruments more often to prevent spatial disorientation. If an autopilot is available, it should be turned on to assist in better aircraft control and keeping the wings level, whenever spatial disorientation is a concern.

• I would wait 12 to 24 hours after scuba diving, depending on if it were a controlled descent or not, to ward off possible nitrogen oxide symptoms.

• I would wait at least 8 hours after drinking alcohol before takeoff.

36. Hazardous weather caused you to delay your return flight home by a few days. As a result, the annual inspection and transponder check are now both out of date. Do regulations permit you to fly home with these items out of date?

Yes, I can legally fly home without the transponder inspection, provided that:

• The transponder is not turned ON.

• An "INOP" sticker is placed near the ON/OFF switch (to indicate inoperative equipment).

• I avoid flight into Class C airspace, above Class C airspace, within 30 NM of Class B airspace, above Class B airspace, anywhere above 10,000 MSL, or

- If flying in airspace normally requiring a transponder, I have the authorization of the air traffic facility chief to operate in airspace without it. (I would call the facility chief on the phone before takeoff.)

Flight without an annual inspection can be initiated only with the issuance of a special flight permit issued by the FSDO. So I can fly home provided I've been issued a permit and am in compliance with the conditions listed on the permit.

37. It's Saturday morning and you are ready for the flight home. During your preflight, you find that the landing light is inoperative. Will this affect your ability to fly home?

Demonstrate your awareness that all installed equipment must be operational on the airplane before takeoff, and the two legal ways to fly with inoperative equipment.

Regulations require that:
- all installed equipment be operational before takeoff, unless:
  › the flight is in compliance with an approved minimum equipment list, or
  › the inoperative equipment is not required by type design, regulations, or airworthiness directives (ADs).
- the pilot can safely operate the airplane without the equipment that has become inoperative.
- the pilot removes or deactivates any inoperative equipment.
- the pilot has placarded any inoperative equipment near the ON/OFF switch.

Because the landing light is not required and I feel that I can safely fly the airplane during the day without it, I will pull the circuit breaker and stick an INOP sticker near the light switch.

38. **You have volunteered to fly a sick child to meet an ambulance at Big Controlled Airport. It's a clear night when at 60 NM out you notice an ammeter discharge. You guess you have about 30 minutes of battery remaining. What will you do?**

There is no right answer; this is simply your opportunity to demonstrate your aeronautical decision making (ADM). You should show a willingness to declare an emergency and divert. Include a discussion of ways to manage the electrical system until landing. Include your thoughts out loud until you make a final decision. You could also mention whether you would you do anything differently if this was a Pilot-N-Paws flight with a sick animal rather than a sick child.

- Within 30 minutes, I might make Big Controlled Airport, but may not be able to communicate with ATC when I get there.

- I could declare an emergency (to obtain radar assistance and priority handling into Big Controlled Airport).

- It might be safer to divert to the "NRST" airport, but then we would miss the ambulance pre-arranged for the patient. I would reduce the electrical load by turning off all unnecessary electrical system equipment. *[Specify the particular cockpit equipment you would turn off in your training airplane.]*

39. After an exhausting three-day business meeting, you are loading up the rental airplane for the two-hour flight home when you discover you have lost your reading glasses. You can see in the distance, but can't read instruments or a chart very easy. The weather is good and if you depart in the next 20 minutes you can be home before dark. What will you do?

There is no right answer; this is simply an opportunity to demonstrate your risk management and aeronautical decision making (ADM). Voice your thought process out loud until you make a final decision.

- I would ask passengers or others (if available) to assist me in searching for my lost glasses.
- If possession of corrective lenses is required on my medical certificate, then a takeoff is not permitted.
- How familiar am I with the rental plane? Can I see "well enough" to fly a plane I don't often fly?
- I could spend the night, buy a new pair of glasses, get some rest, and depart fresh in the morning.

Maneuvers Table

Appendix 1

Appendix 1

Private Pilot Airman Certification Standards (condensed)

Task	Objective Minimum acceptable standard of performance
Takeoff Normal/Crosswind Short/Soft	V_Y +10 / -5 V_X +10 / -5, then V_Y +10 / -5
Landing Normal/Crosswind Forward Slip Short Soft Go Around	1.3 V_{S0} +10 / -5, touch at or within 400 feet beyond target Min float, touch at or within 400 feet beyond target 1.3 V_{S0} +10 / -5, touch at or within 200 feet beyond target 1.3 V_{S0} +10 / -5, touch at minimum speed and descent rate Power (Carb Heat off?), pitch for V_Y +10 / -5, flaps, gear
Emergency Operations Emergency Approach and Landing	Use recommended descent configuration and airspeed ±10 kts.

		Heading or bank ±°	Altitude ± ft	Speed ± kts
Traffic Pattern	Accurate track and safe spacing		100	10
Pilotage/NAV/Diverting	Know position ± 3 NM	15	200	ETA ±5min

Instrument Flying
   Straight and level
   Constant airspeed climb and
    descend
   Turns and rollouts on heading
   Communications, Navigation,
    Radar Services
   Recovery from unusual
    attitudes
	
	Recover to stabilized
	flight w/o excesses
		
		20
		20
		
		10
		20
			
			200
			200
			
			200
			200
				
				10
				10
				
				10
				10

*Slow Flight and Stalls (no flight
   below 1,500 AGL)*
Power-off Stalls
 	
Power-on Stalls
 	
Maneuvering during Slow Flight
   Straight & level, turns, climbs,
   descents
	
	S & L or max. 20° bank
	Full-stall then recover
	
	S & L or max. 20° bank
	Full-stall then recover
		
		10
		
		10
		
		10
			
			100
				
				MCA
				+10/-0

Performance Maneuvers
Steep turns
   360° with 45° ±5° bank,
   coordinated
		10	100	10

Ground Reference Maneuvers	Remain 600–1,000 AGL		100	10

Exam Tip: Remember to always perform "clearing turns" prior to beginning any flight maneuver.

Appendix 1

Applicant's Practical Test Checklist

Appendix 2

Applicant's Practical Test Checklist

Appointment with Evaluator _____

Evaluator's Name _____

Location _____

Date/Time _____

Acceptable Aircraft

Aircraft Documents

___ Airworthiness Certificate

___ Registration Certificate

___ Operating Limitations

Aircraft Maintenance Records

___ Logbook Record of Airworthiness Inspections and AD Compliance

___ Pilot's Operating Handbook, FAA-Approved Airplane Flight Manual

___ Current Weight and Balance Data

Personal Equipment

___ View-Limiting Device

___ Current Aeronautical Charts (printed or electronic)

___ Computer and Plotter

___ Flight Plan Form and Flight Logs (printed or electronic)

___ *Chart Supplements U.S.*, Airport Diagrams and appropriate publications

___ Current AIM

Personal Records

___ Identification — Photo/Signature ID

___ Pilot Certificate

___ Current Medical Certificate

___ Completed FAA Form 8710-1, Airman Certificate and/or Rating Application with Instructor's Signature (or IACRA equivalent with Applicant's FTN and Application ID)

___ Original Knowledge Test Report

___ Pilot Logbook with Appropriate Instructor Endorsements

Continued

___FAA Form 8060-5, Notice of Disapproval (if applicable)

___Letter of Discontinuance (if applicable)

___Approved School Graduation Certificate (if applicable)

___Evaluator's Fee (if applicable)

Operations of Aircraft Without/ With an MEL

Appendix 3

Operations of Aircraft *Without* a Minimum Equipment List (MEL)

(14 CFR 91.213, AC 91-67, fsims.faa.gov 8900.1)

During the preflight inspection, the pilot discovers inoperative instruments or equipment.

DECISION SEQUENCE:

1. **Are the inoperative instruments or equipment part of the VFR-day type certification?** (14 CFR 91.213(d)(2)(i))

   These are the instruments and equipment prescribed in the applicable airworthiness regulations under which the aircraft was type-certificated (14 CFR Part 23 for newer aircraft and CAR Part 3 for much older aircraft).

   Note: Referencing the aircraft certification regulations to determine if instruments and equipment are required can be a complex task. In general, the instruments and equipment required by the aircraft certification regulations can be found in the aircraft's Equipment List and Type Certificate Data Sheet (TCDS).

   If YES, the aircraft is not airworthy and maintenance is required before you can fly.

   If NO, go to next the step.

2. **Are the inoperative instruments or equipment listed as "Required" on the aircraft's equipment list, or "kinds of operations equipment list" (KOEL) for the kind of flight operation being conducted?** (14 CFR 91.213 (d)(2)(ii))

   Note: Many newer aircraft have a "Kinds of Operations" equipment list which refers to the kinds of operations (VFR Day, VFR Night, IFR Day, IFR Night, Icing) in which the aircraft can operate. The equipment list and KOEL are located in the AFM.

   If YES, the aircraft is not airworthy and maintenance is required before you can fly.

   If NO, go to next the step.

3. **Are the inoperative instruments or equipment required by 14 CFR §91.205, 91.207, or any other rule of 14 CFR Part 91 for the specific kind of flight operation being conducted?** (14 CFR 91.213(d)(2)(iii))

   Note: Other required equipment regulations include: 91.205 VFR Day, VFR Night, IFR; 91.207 – ELTs; 91.209 – Aircraft Lights; 91.215 – ATC Transponders.

   If YES, the aircraft is not airworthy and maintenance is required before you can fly.

   If NO, go to the next step.

4. **Are the inoperative instruments or equipment required to be operational by an Airworthiness Directive (AD)? Check the aircraft maintenance logs and/or consult with a maintenance technician to determine AD compliance.** (14 CFR 91.213(d)(2)(iv))

   If YES, the aircraft is not airworthy and maintenance is required before you can fly.

   If NO, go to the next step.

5. **At this point, the inoperative instruments or equipment must be:**

   REMOVED from the aircraft (14 CFR 91.213(d)(3)(i)), the cockpit control placarded, and the maintenance record (logbook) updated in accordance with 14 CFR 43.9.

   OR

   DEACTIVATED and PLACARDED "Inoperative"(14 CFR 91.213(d)(3)(ii). If deactivation of the inoperative instrument or equipment involves maintenance, it must be accomplished and recorded in accordance with 14 CFR Part 43.

6. **Finally, a determination is made by a certificated and appropriately rated pilot or mechanic that the inoperative instrument or equipment does not constitute a hazard to the aircraft for the anticipated conditions of the flight, e.g., day VFR, night VFR etc.**

Operations of Aircraft *With* a Minimum Equipment List (MEL)

(14 CFR 91.213, AC 91-67, fsims.faa.gov 8900.1)

During the preflight inspection, the pilot discovers inoperative instruments or equipment.

DECISION SEQUENCE:

1. **Is the inoperative equipment not included in the MEL, but required by the type certification, AD or other special conditions?**

   If YES, the aircraft is not airworthy and maintenance is required before flight.

   If NO, go to next step.

2. **The pilot performs or has a qualified person perform the appropriate "O" or "M" deactivation or removal procedure.**

   Note: Two categories of maintenance procedures:

   "O" Operations procedures—can be performed by pilot; must be accomplished before or during operation with listed item of equipment inoperative.

   "M" Maintenance procedures—must be done by maintenance personnel and be accomplished before beginning operation with the listed item of equipment inoperative.

3. **The pilot or maintenance personnel placards the inoperative equipment and updates the maintenance record (logbook).**

4. **The pilot confirms that the inoperative equipment does not present hazards to the conditions of flight.**